Scarab Arts Annual
Volume Three

Edited by Charles Alexander, Treena Flannery Ericson, Bridgett Ritz and VATO

Scarab Club • Detroit • 2011

The Scarab Club
217 Farnsworth
Detroit, MI 48202
http://www.scarabclub.org

ISBN 978-1-105-20174-5

Printed in the U.S.

Front cover art: Reception Desk, ca. 1922, by Alfred Nygard, carved, polychromed gumwood, gift of the artist, collection of the Scarab Club, photographed by Vincent Verna. Back cover art: Michigan Historical Marker photographed by VATO.

This book is dedicated to all members of the Scarab Club, past and present.

FOREWARD

The City of Detroit continues to be a lightning rod of conversation as the United States and global community struggle economically. Fox News political commentator Glenn Beck stirred Metro Detroit's emotions as he compared our city to post-atomic bomb Hiroshima and then went on to comment about how the devastated Japanese city recovered while Detroit lays in waste. Detroit mayor David Bing responded by offering to take Beck on a personal tour of the city. Speaking of mayors, the once promising political leader Kwame Kilpatrick was released on August 2, 2011, from his second incarceration, casting another shadow over his legacy and troubled administration.

Before you is the third installment of the Scarab Club Arts Annual, and it stands as an unwavering testament to the Scarab Club's commitment to this important project and the ongoing collective effort in documenting and preserving the Detroit art scene during these years of great interest. It is the goal of the club to continue the Annual for many years to come. The purpose of the Annual is to provide Scarab Club member artists and poets an opportunity to have their work published in book form. Since participation in this publication is on a volunteer basis, the images and words found in the Annual are not a complete representation of all the Scarab Club members. An undertaking of this size owes a debt to many. They are, in no particular order, VATO (Aric Tosqui) and Susan Higman Larsen for spearheading the project; the front office staff, Christine Renner, executive director, and Treena Flannery Ericson, gallery director, who supported this effort by handling a myriad of tasks, including sending out Annual-related communications and helping answer Annual-related questions and routing submissions; Bridgett Ritz, who again designed the book's handsome layout; and to the Lounge Committee—Charles Alexander and VATO—who vetted the many submissions for this year's Annual.

The Annual was not the club's only notable accomplishments during the 2011 calendar year. Lester Johnson, a Detroit artist and longtime fine arts professor at the College for Creative Studies, joined the ranks of the second floor beam signers, which includes such art notables as Juliana Force, Pablo Davis, Reginald Marsh, and Marcel Duchamp. Johnson holds a BFA and MFA degree from the University of Michigan. His work has been shown in many prestigious galleries and museums, such as the Whitney Museum of American Art and the Detroit Institute of Arts.

2011 also marked the second successful year of *American Aesthetic: Clyde Burroughs Dinner/Lecture Series on American Art and Design*. Distinguished speakers included Margaret Caldwell, Janice Mann, Paul Staiti, and MaryAnn Wilkinson, all of whom are experts in their field.

Artist member Eric Law won the club's highest honor, the Gold Medal, for his photograph *Cattails* during the 97th Annual Gold Medal Exhibition (2010), held in December. The Scarab Club was also awarded much needed grant money from the following organizations: the Kresge Foundation, Erb Foundation, Michigan Council for the Arts and Cultural Affairs, and the National Endowment for the Arts. These granting institutions truly help us continue our mission to serve and educate the arts community of Southeast Michigan and beyond.

These achievements will certainly make us proud as Scarab Club members and further advance our club's 104-year legacy (for more information on the history of the Scarab Club, see *Images of America: The Scarab Club*, 2006). It is my humble belief that significant deceased Scarab Club members such as Mary Jane Bostick, James Swan, Myron Barlow, and Henry T. Ewald, just to name a few, are looking down and smiling proudly on our efforts to further our beloved club. We hope you enjoy volume three of the Scarab Club Arts Annual; it continues to document the Detroit arts community during these unique and changing times, and it is our distinct footprint that we leave for future generations to follow.

Michael Crane
Scarab Club member at large

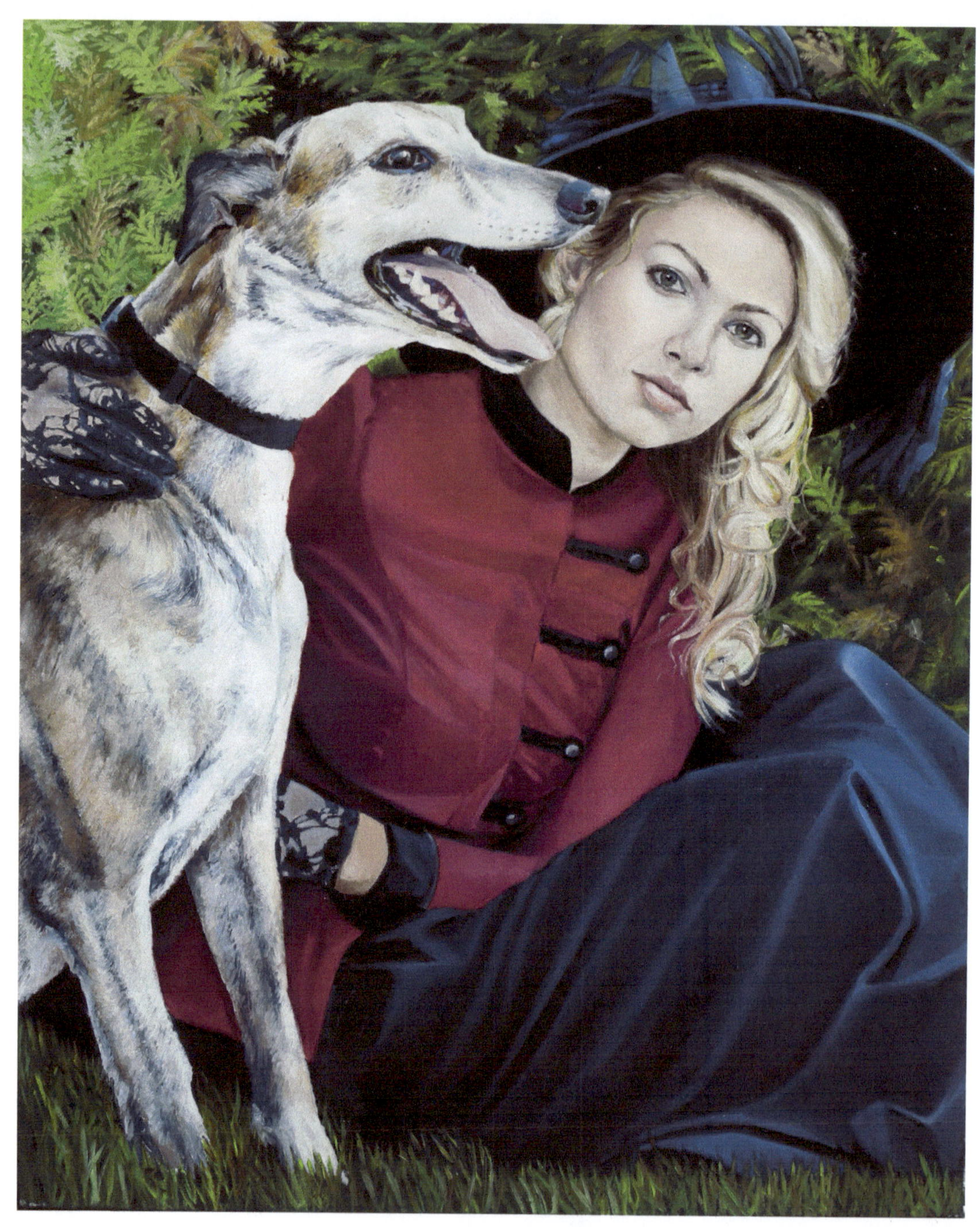

Warm Summer Days, Bill Murcko

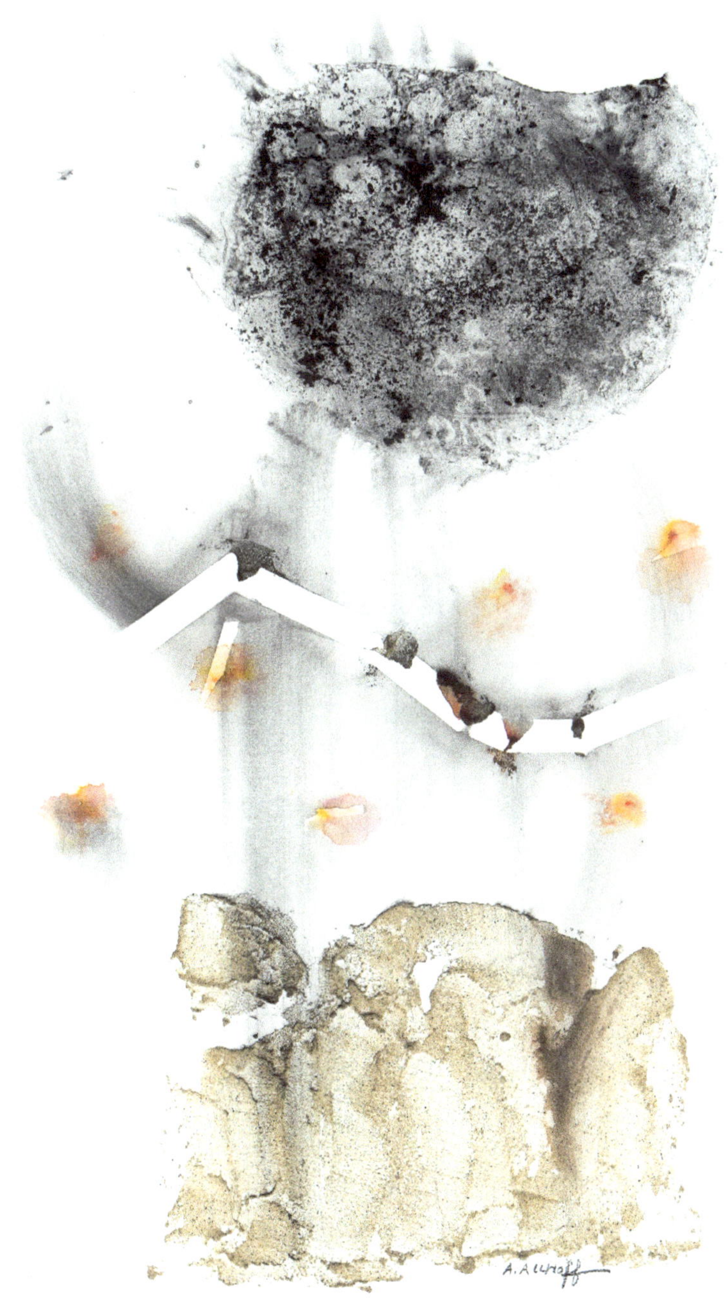

Finale - Organic Faceoff, Alice Allhoff

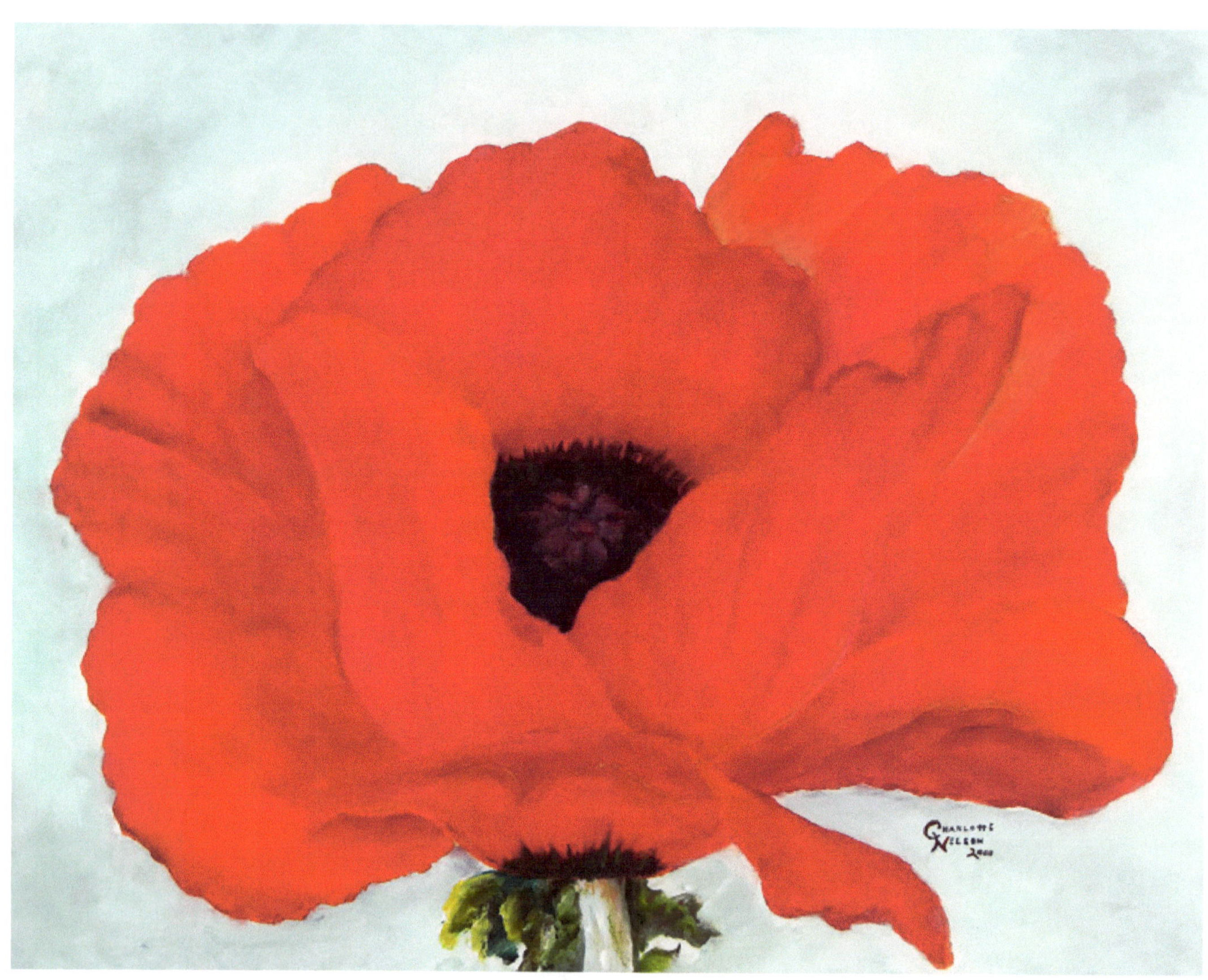

Poppy, Charlotte Nelson

Cattail, Eric Law

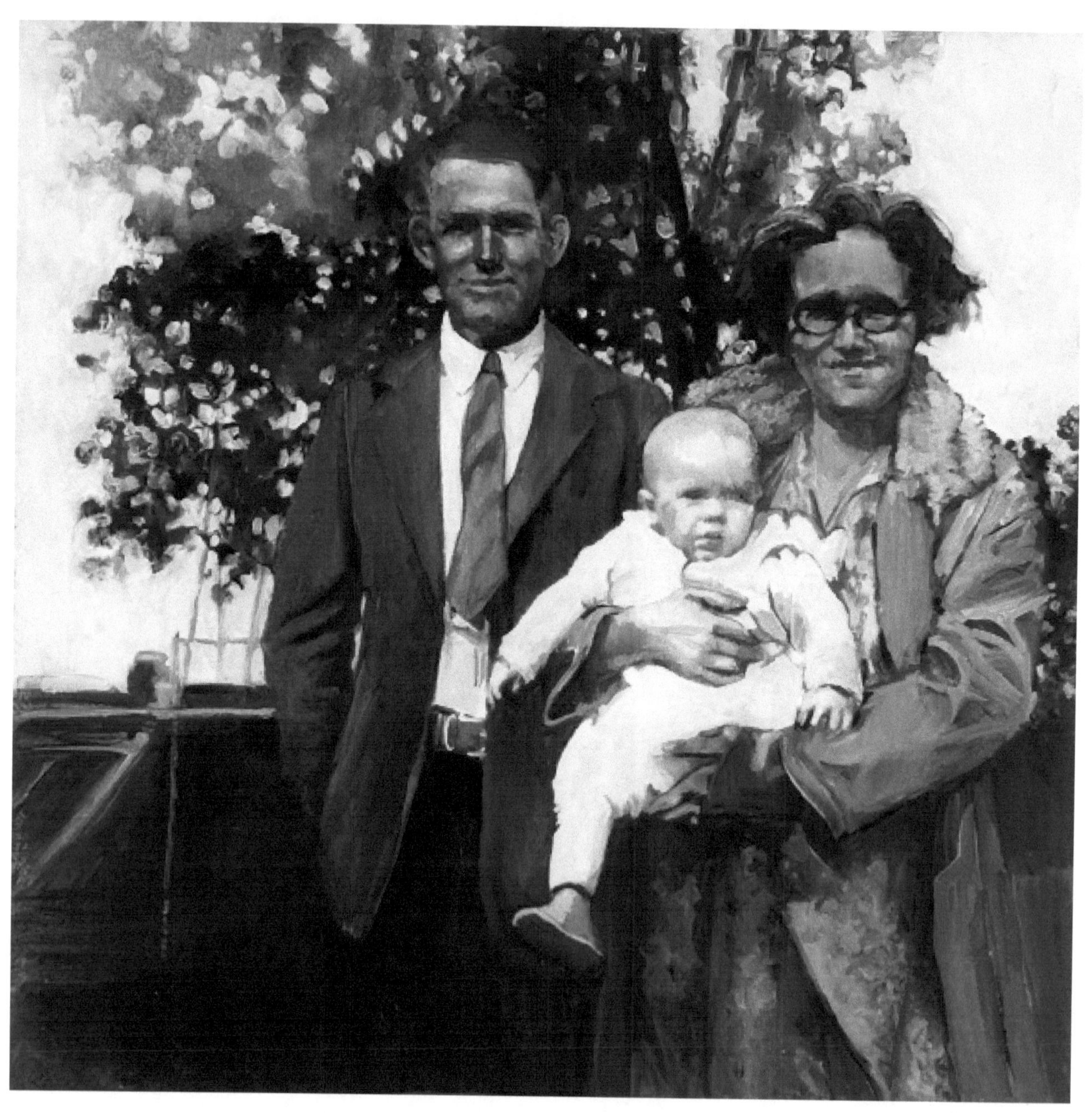

Family, Jeanne Bieri

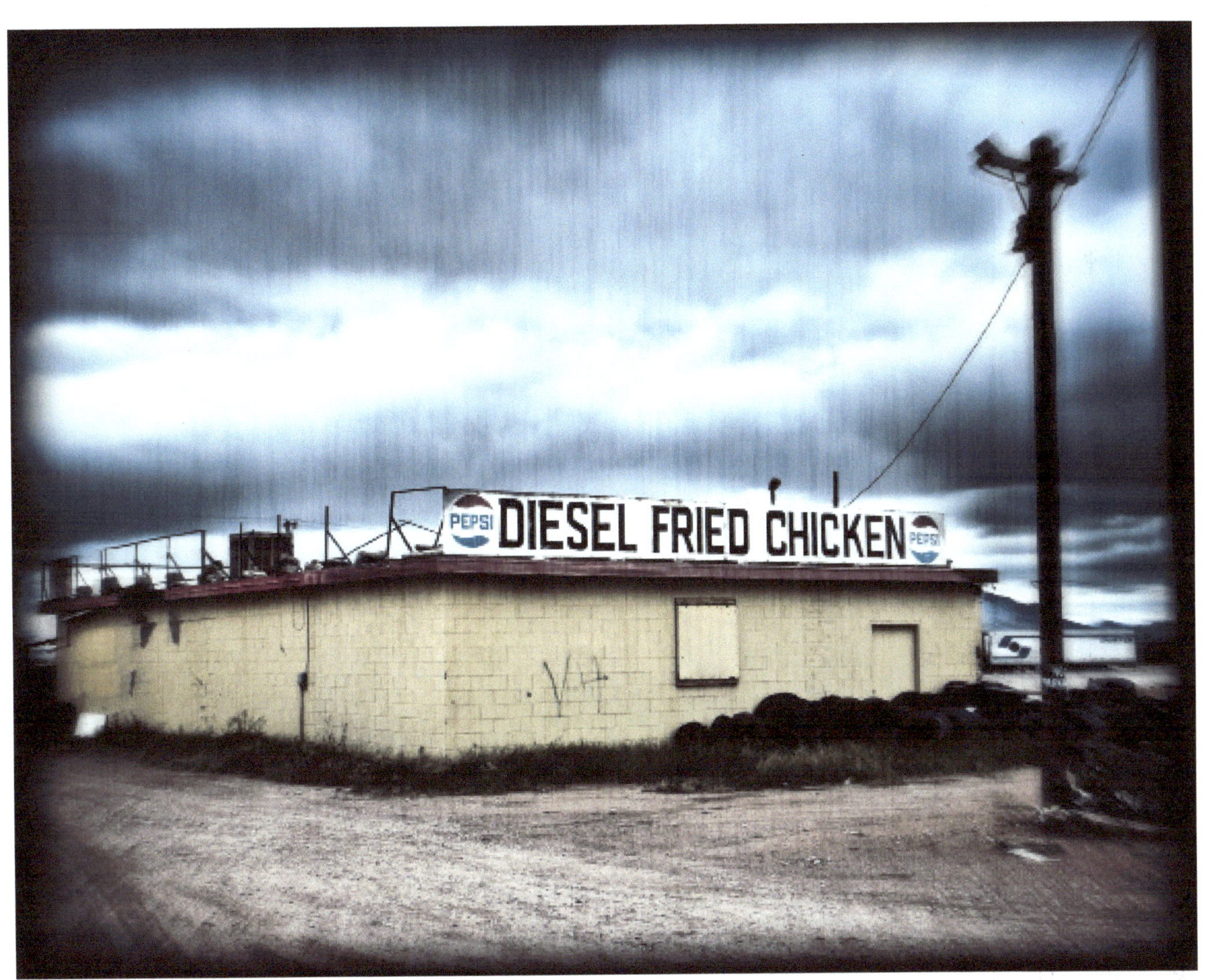

Diesel Fried Chicken, VATO

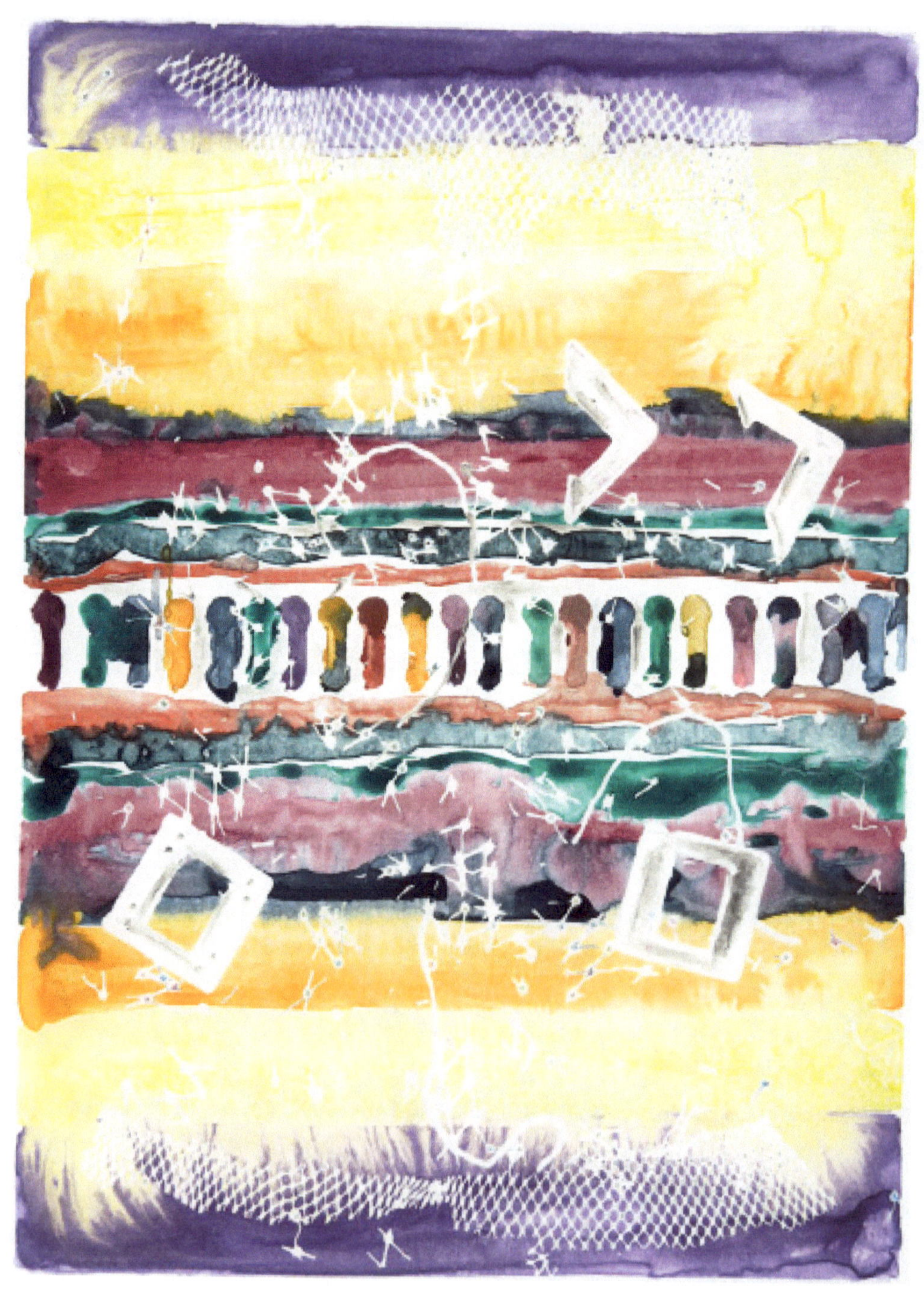

Exodus, Jean Thomas

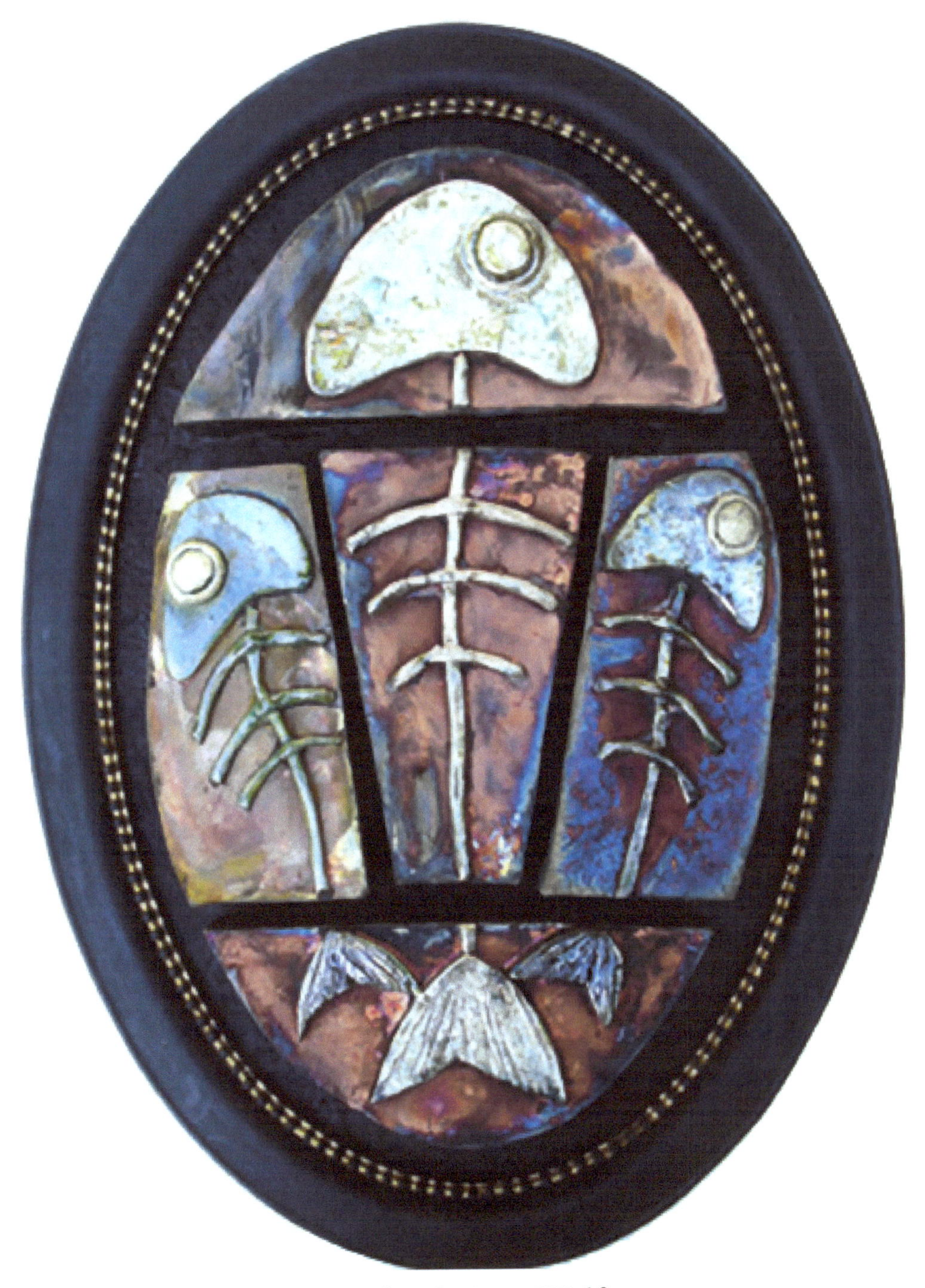

Oval Fish, Amy Wolfe

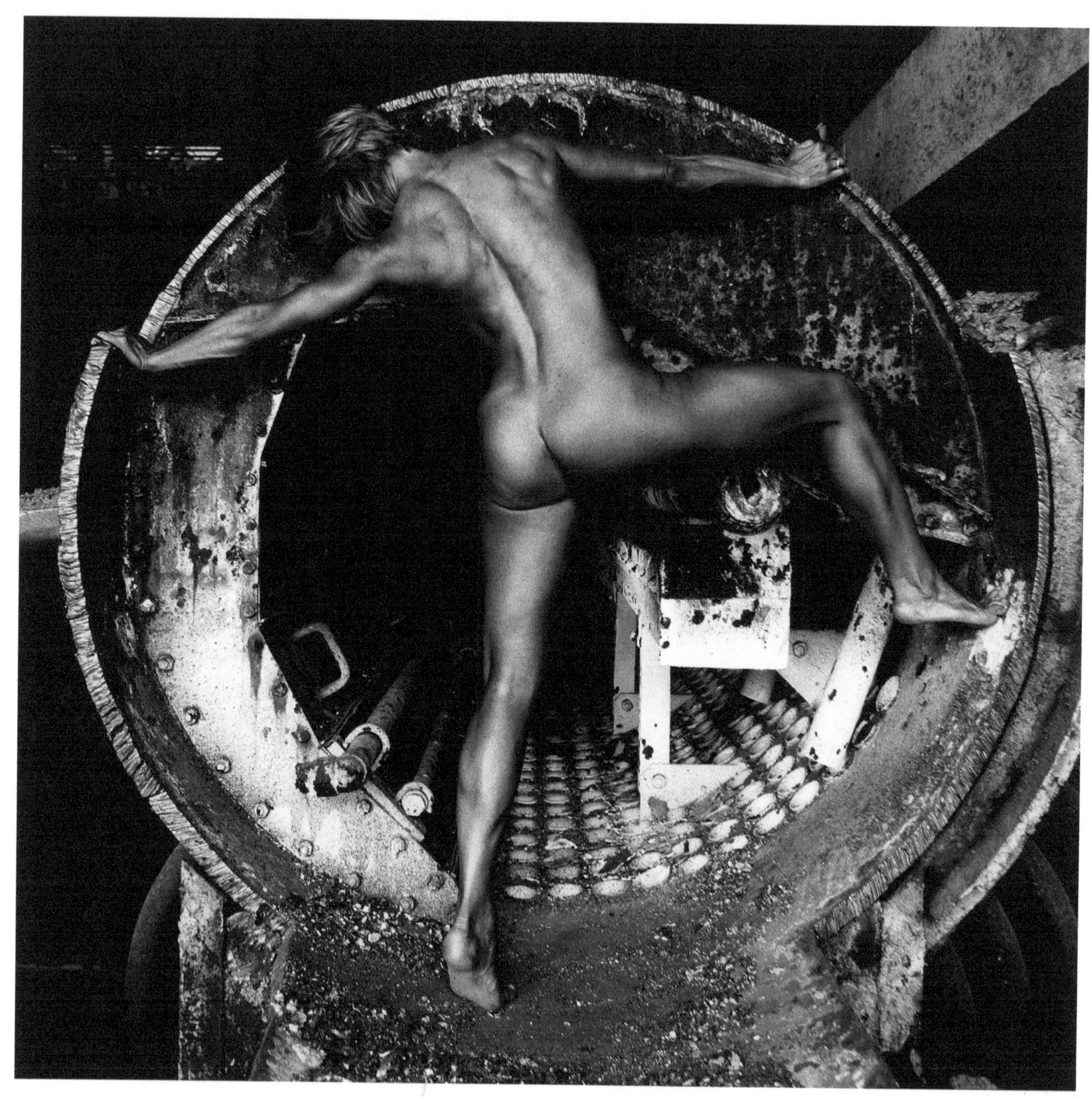

Machine, Gary Mitchell

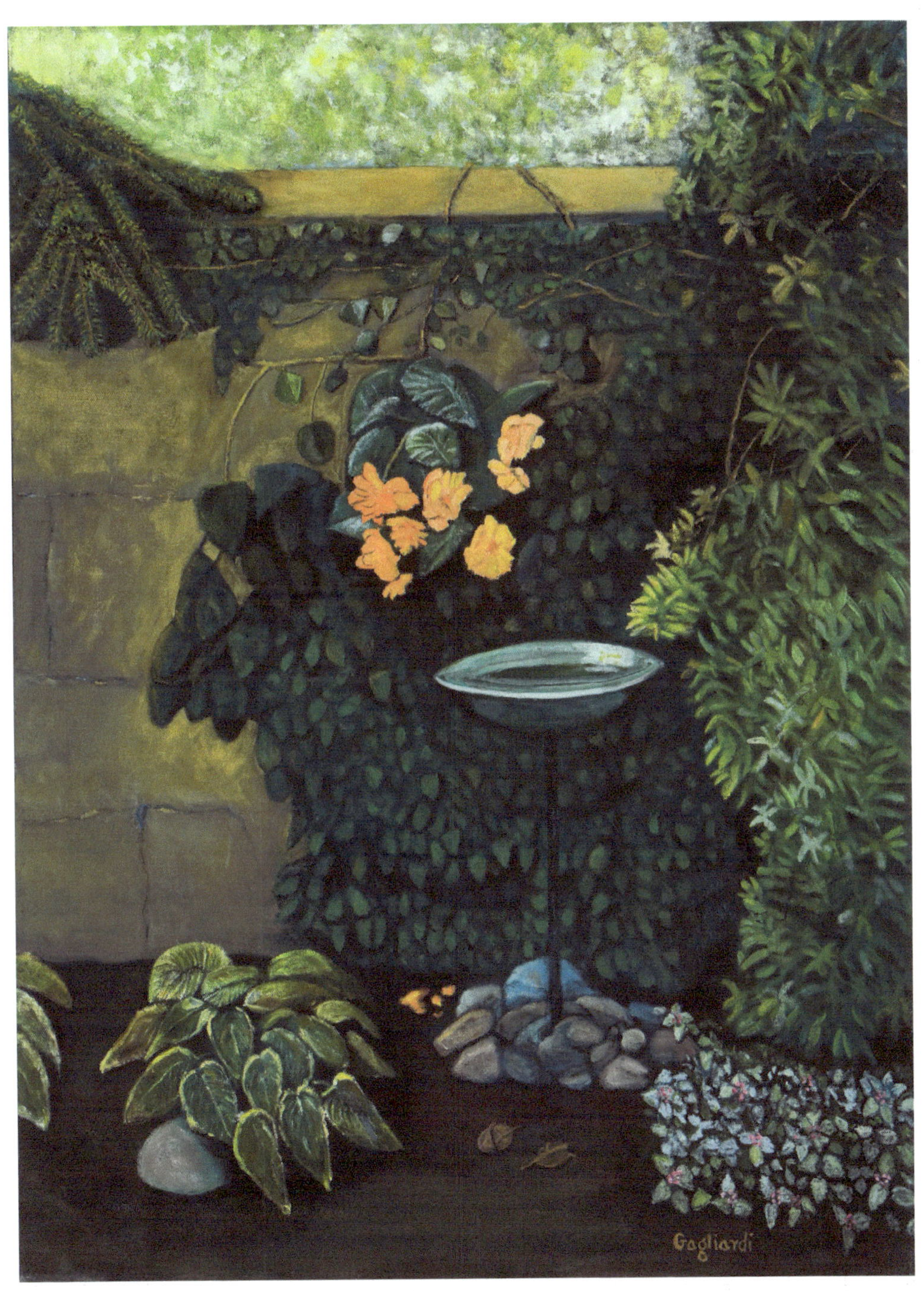

Begonias and Bird Bath, Anthony V. Gagliardi

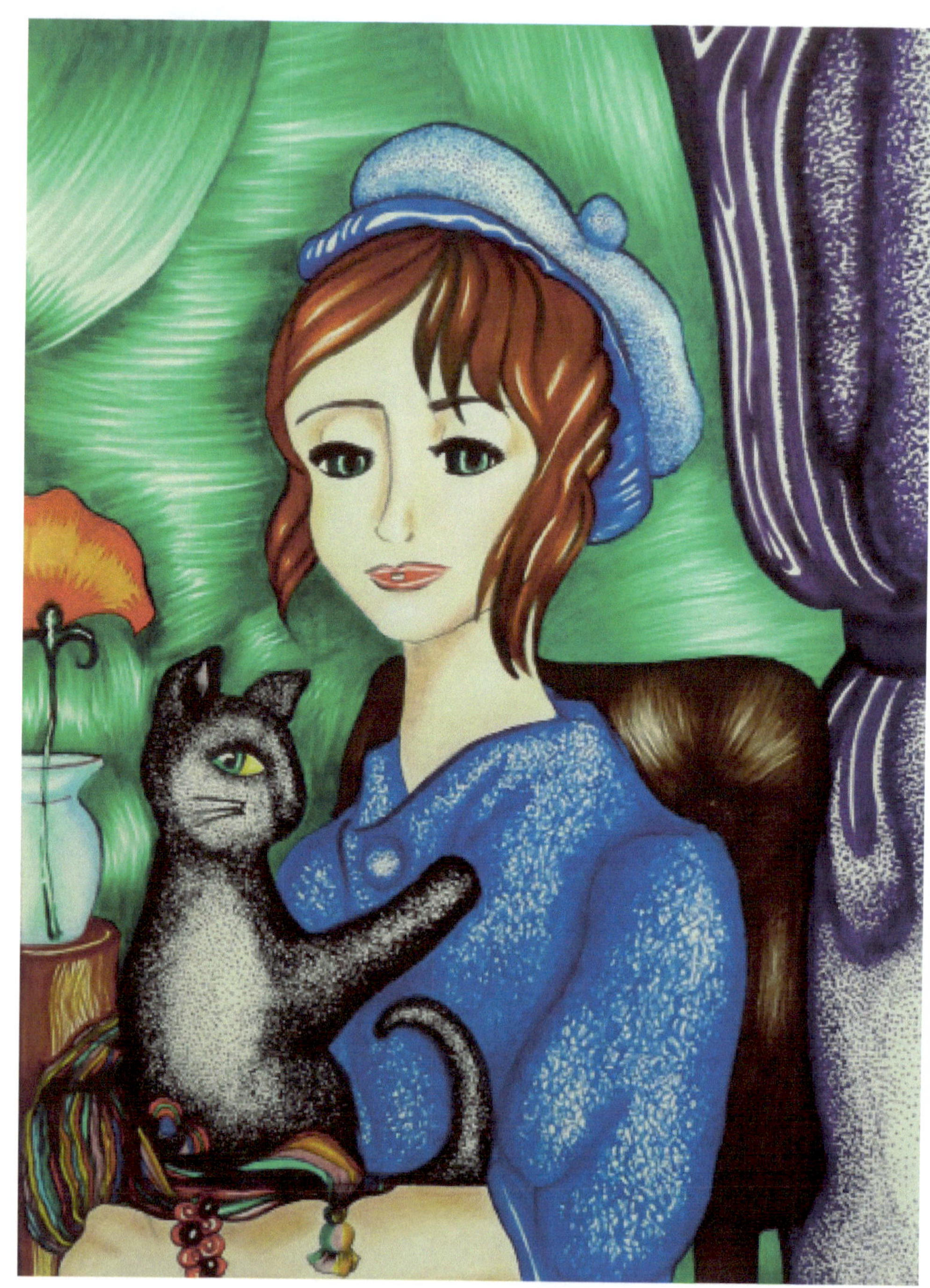

Girl with Her Cat, Abigail Davidson

DANCING WITH DONNA SUMMER

Ellen Hildreth

Under the mirror ball
Two Divas meet
Flashing lights
Blazing eyes
Recognize
The beat
The heat
Never Dies
If you just
Keep dancing

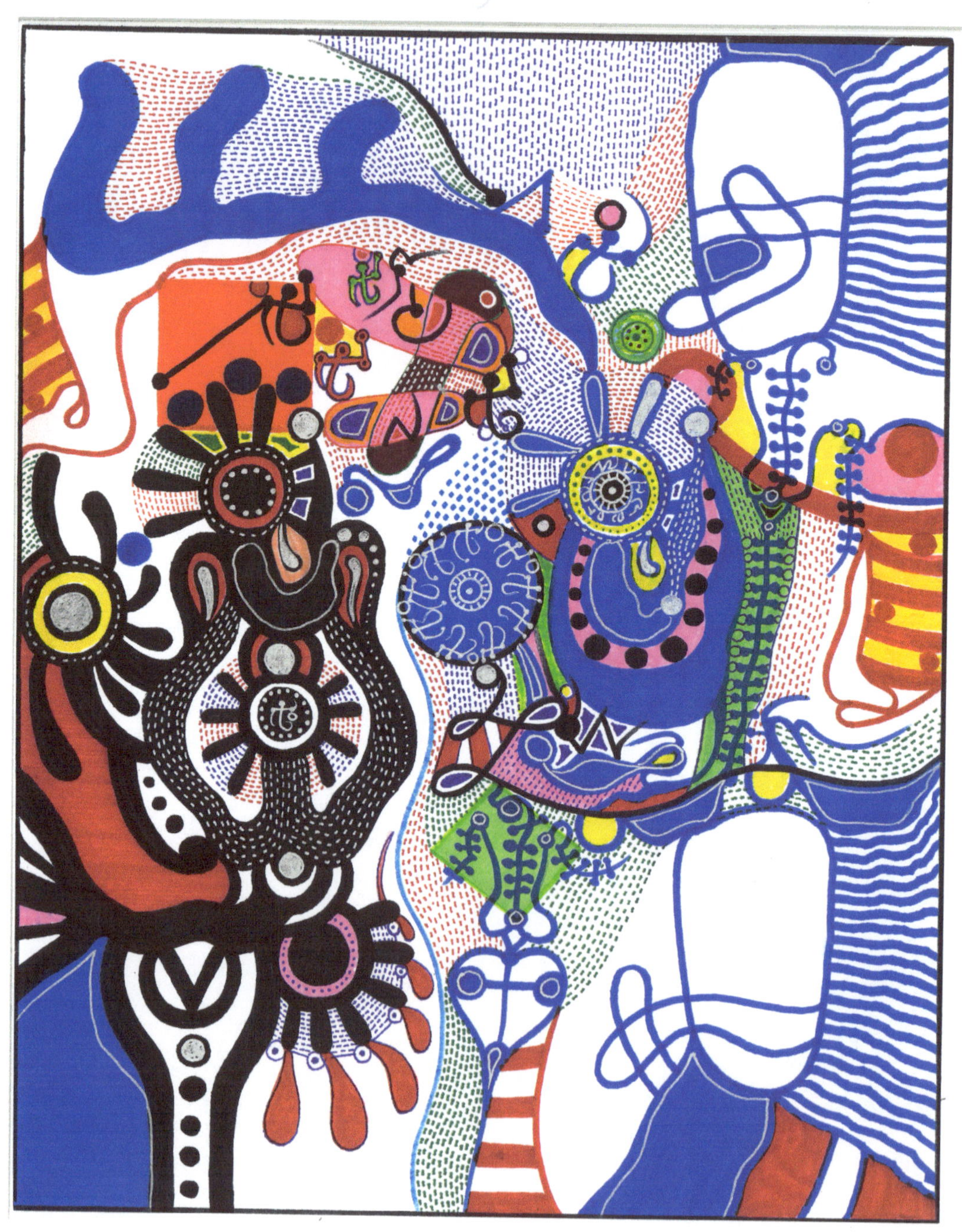

Blue Wave Lengths, Charles Alexander

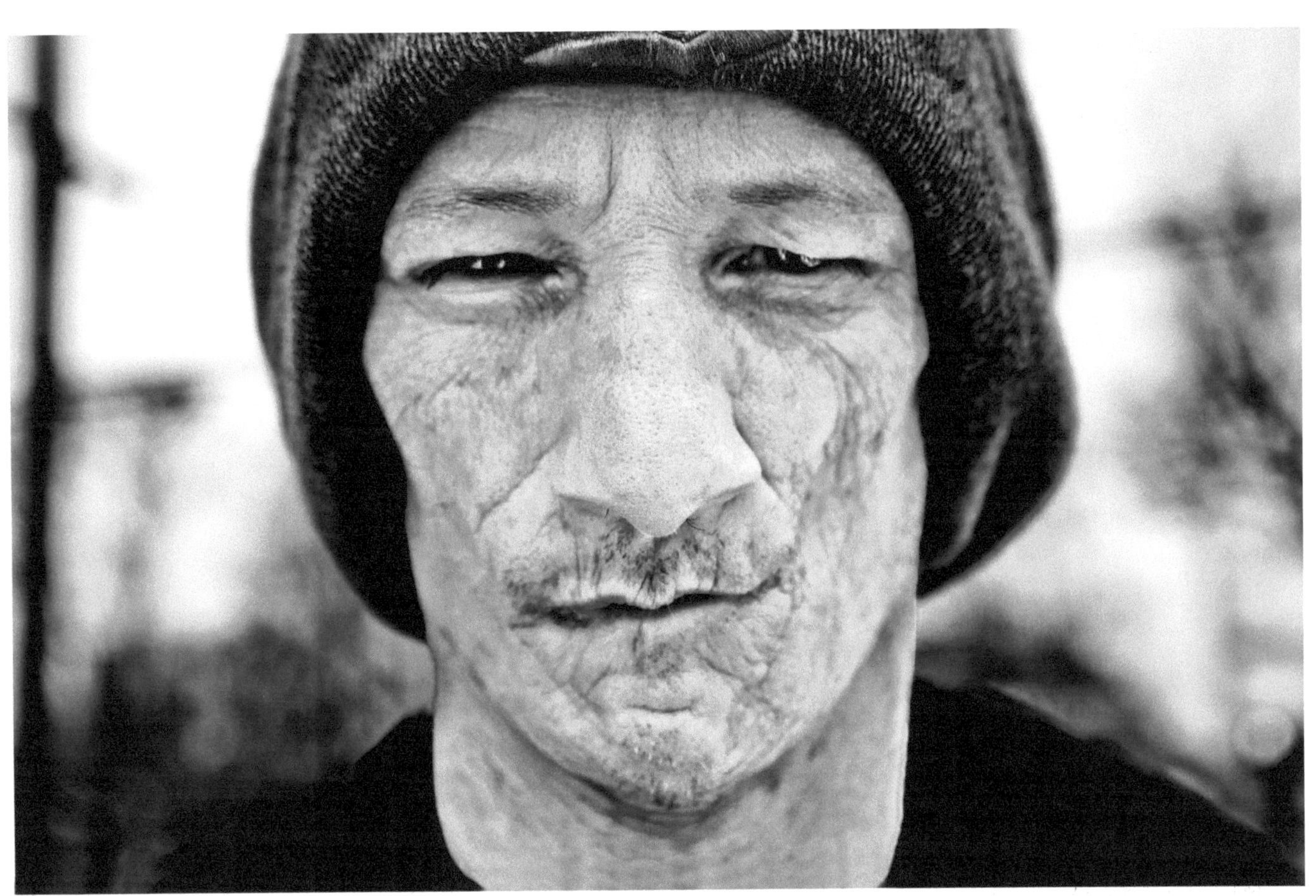

Chuck, Bruce Giffin

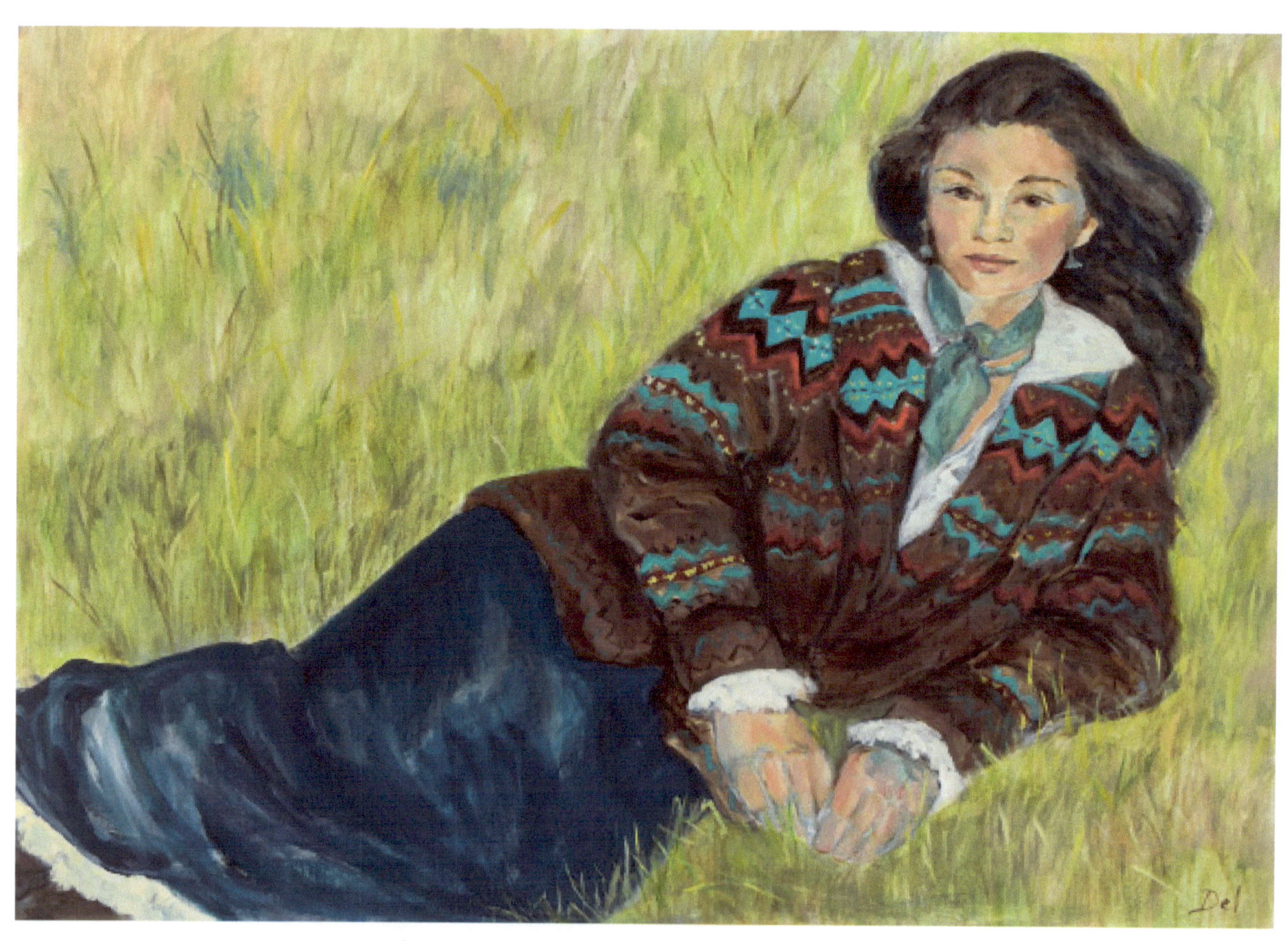

Girl in the Meadow, Delphine Iwankowski

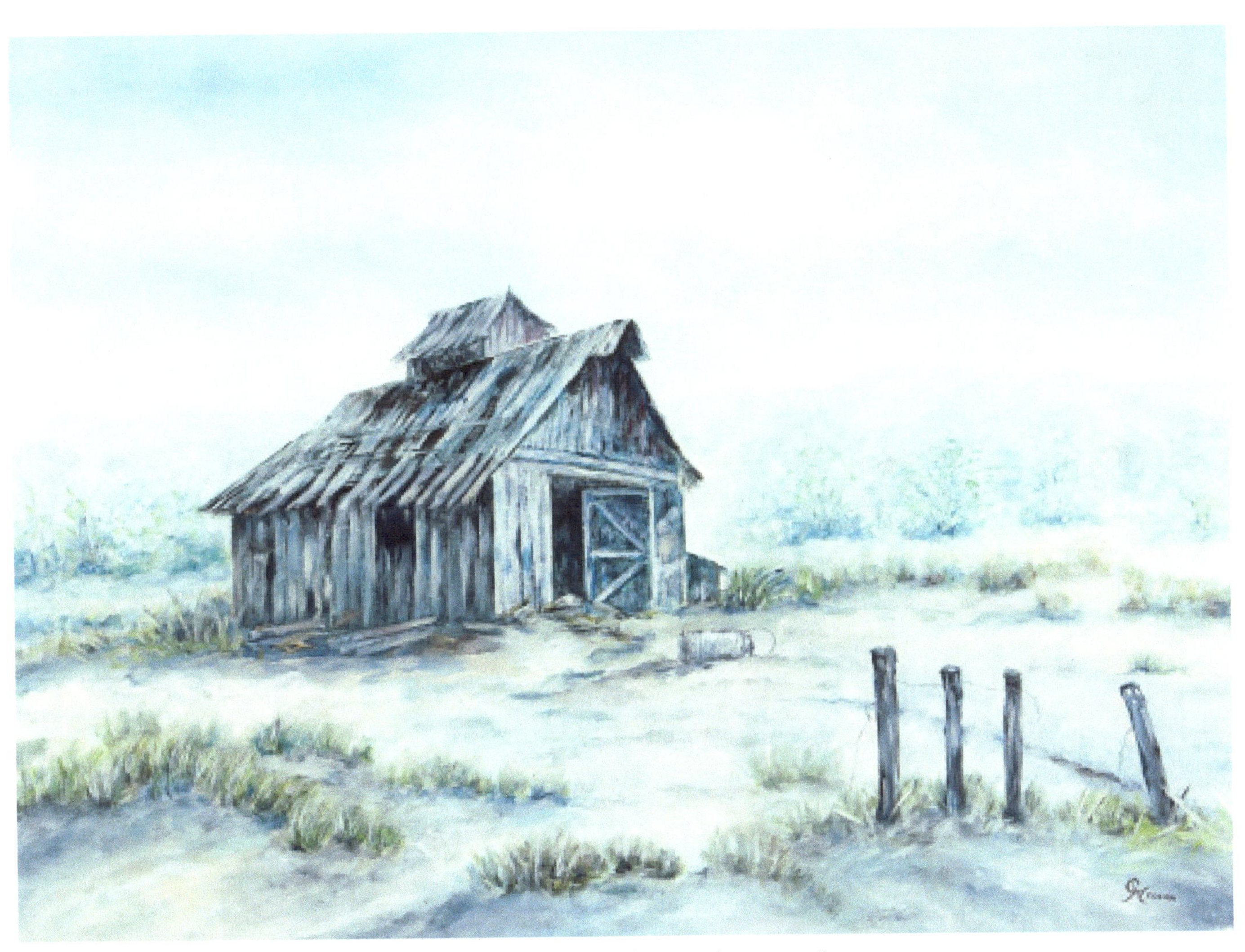

Desolate Dilapidated, Charlotte Nelson

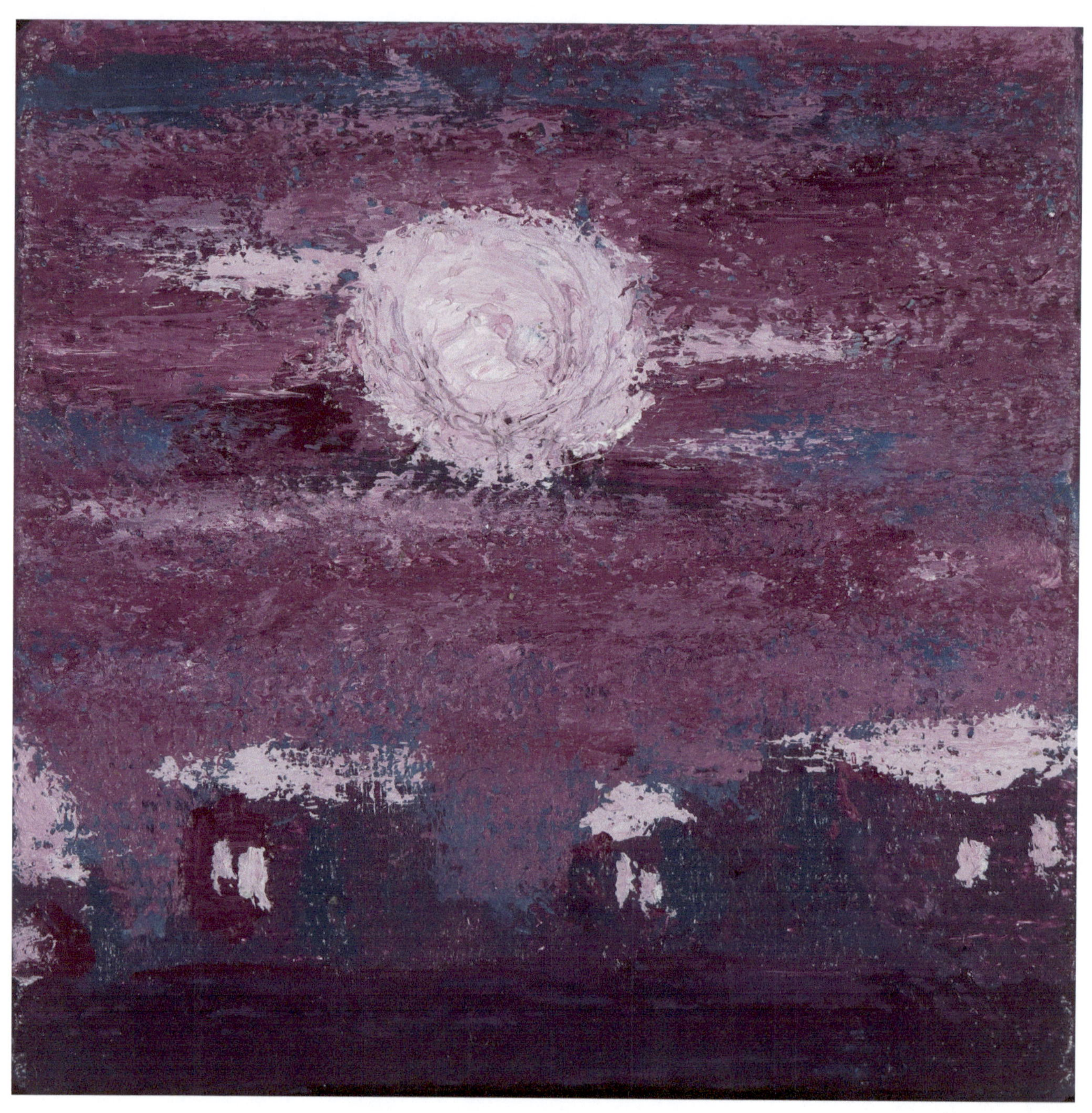

Adobe Village, Carolyn Keith

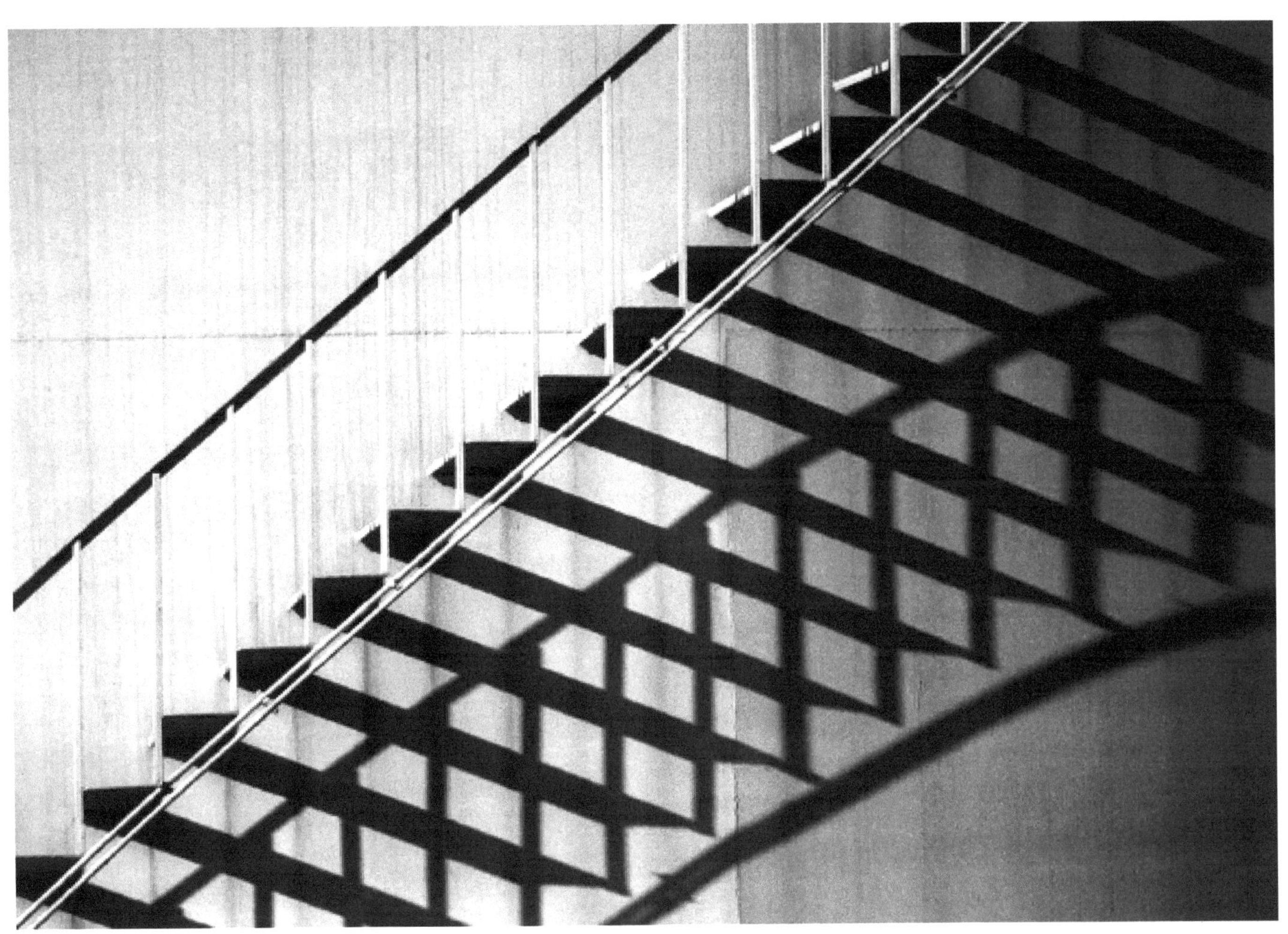

Off I-75, Donna Cyrbok

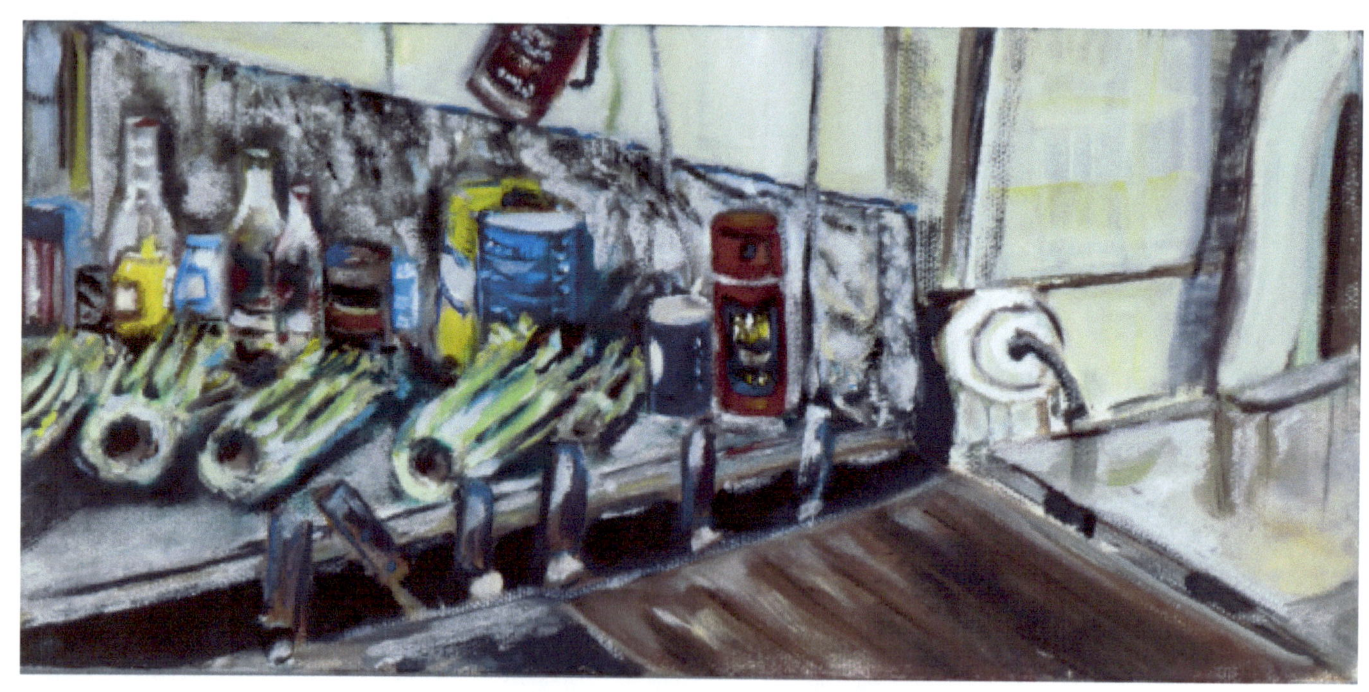

Celery and Raid, Agnes Gira

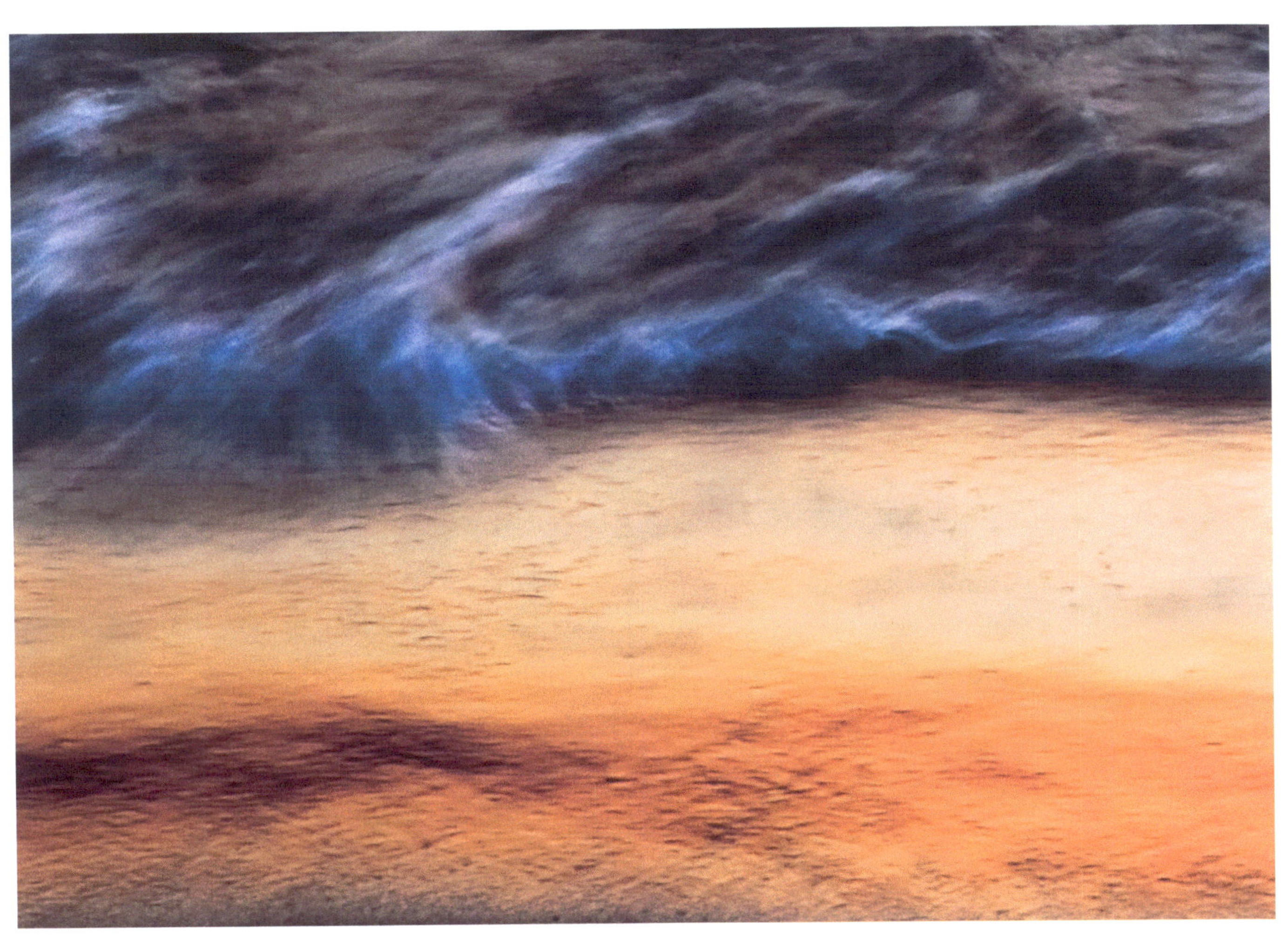

Sandset V, Beverly Benson Wolf

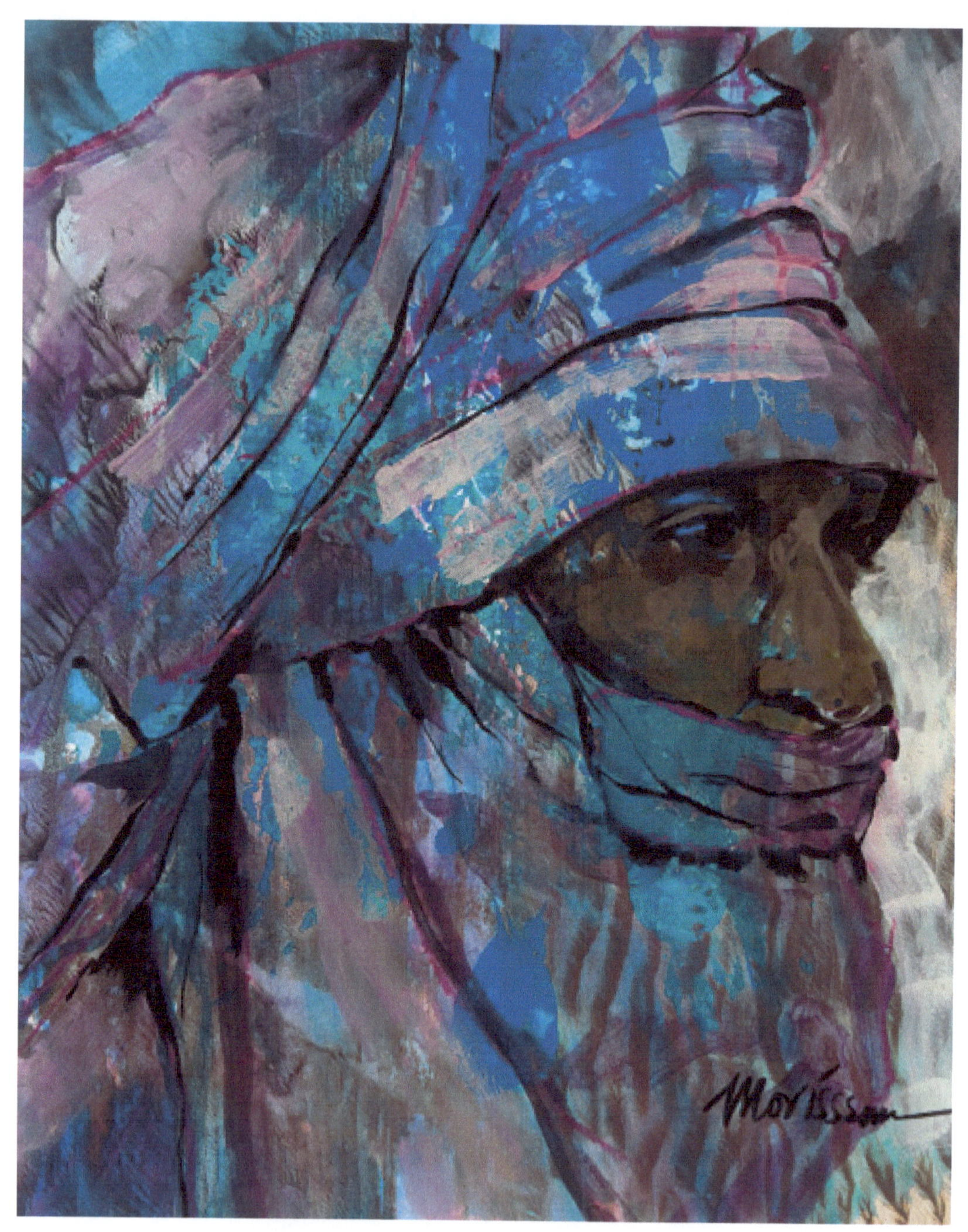

Tuareg Man, Carole Morisseau

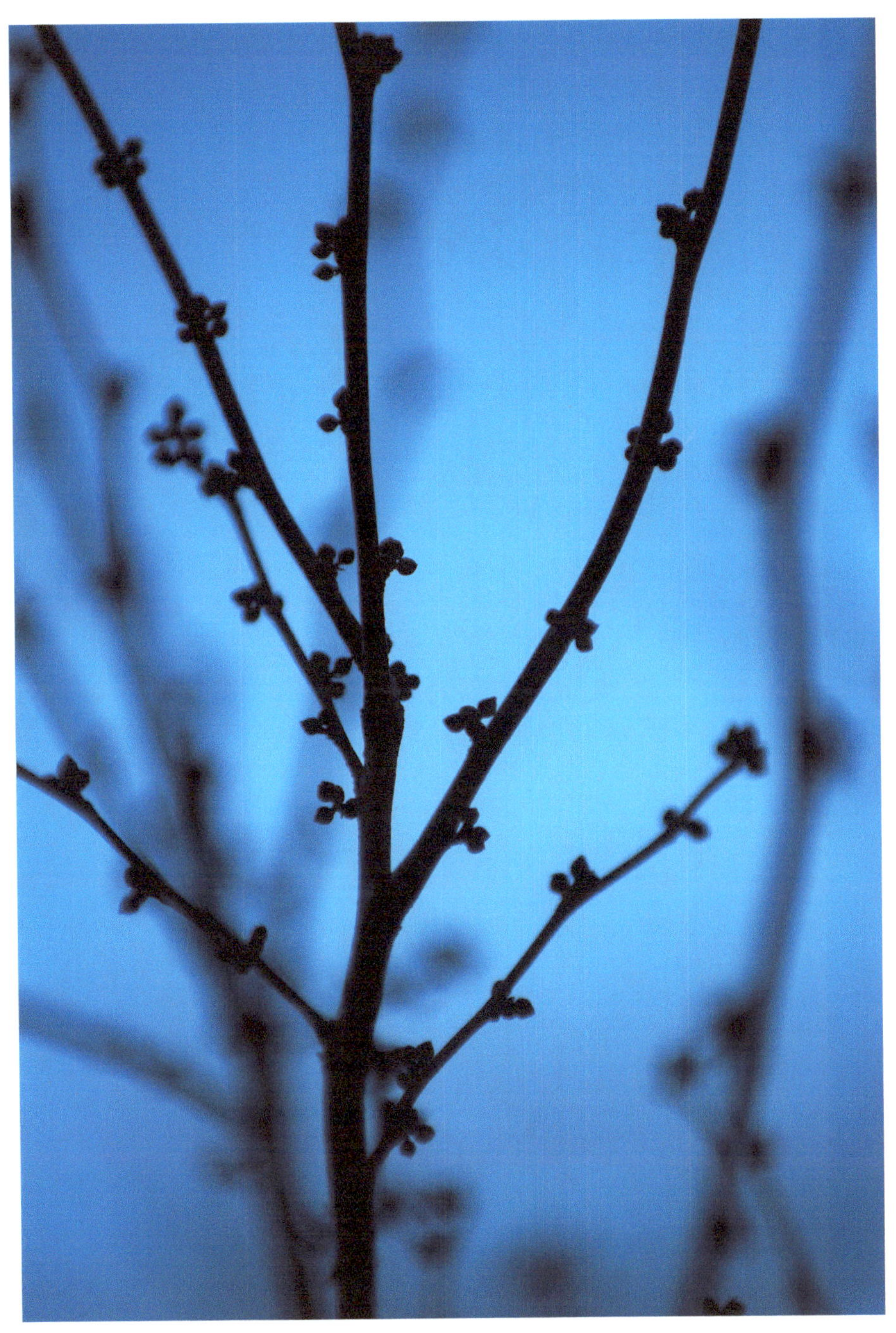

Soft Like Night, Terri Light

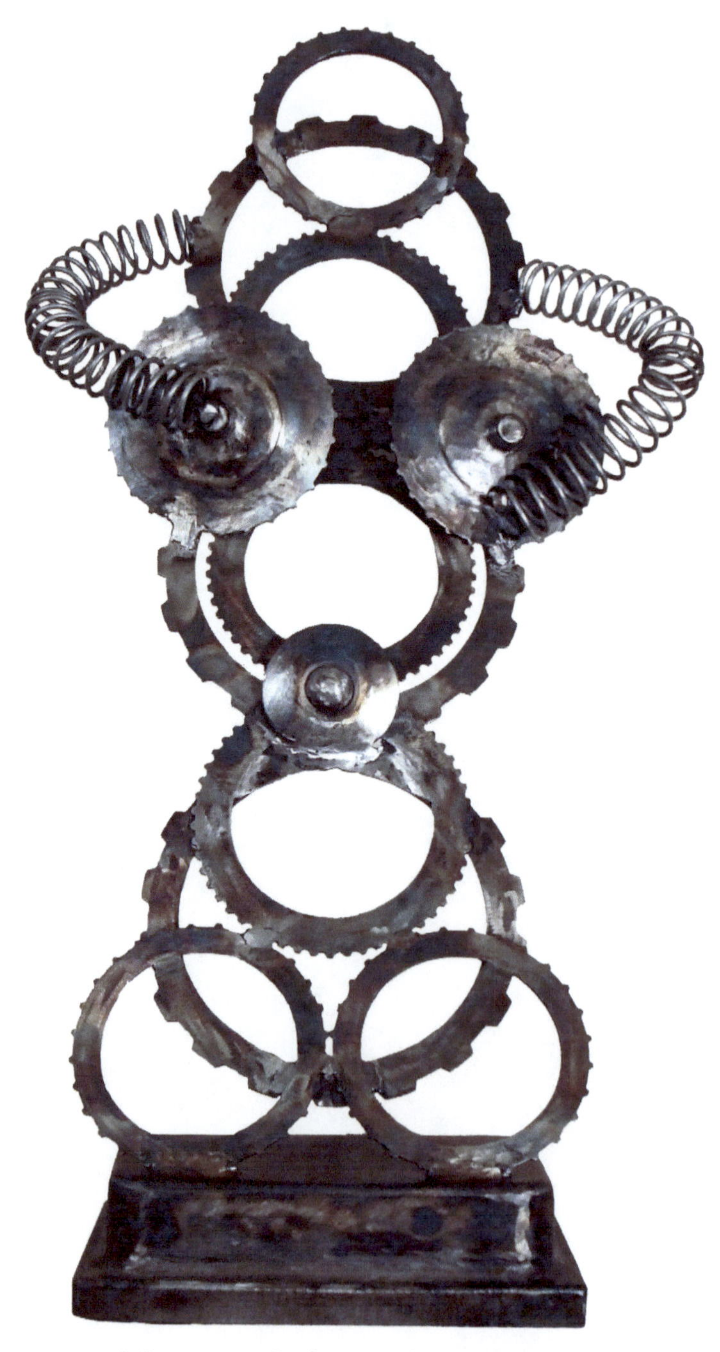

Motorcity Girl, Viorel "Vic" Lupu

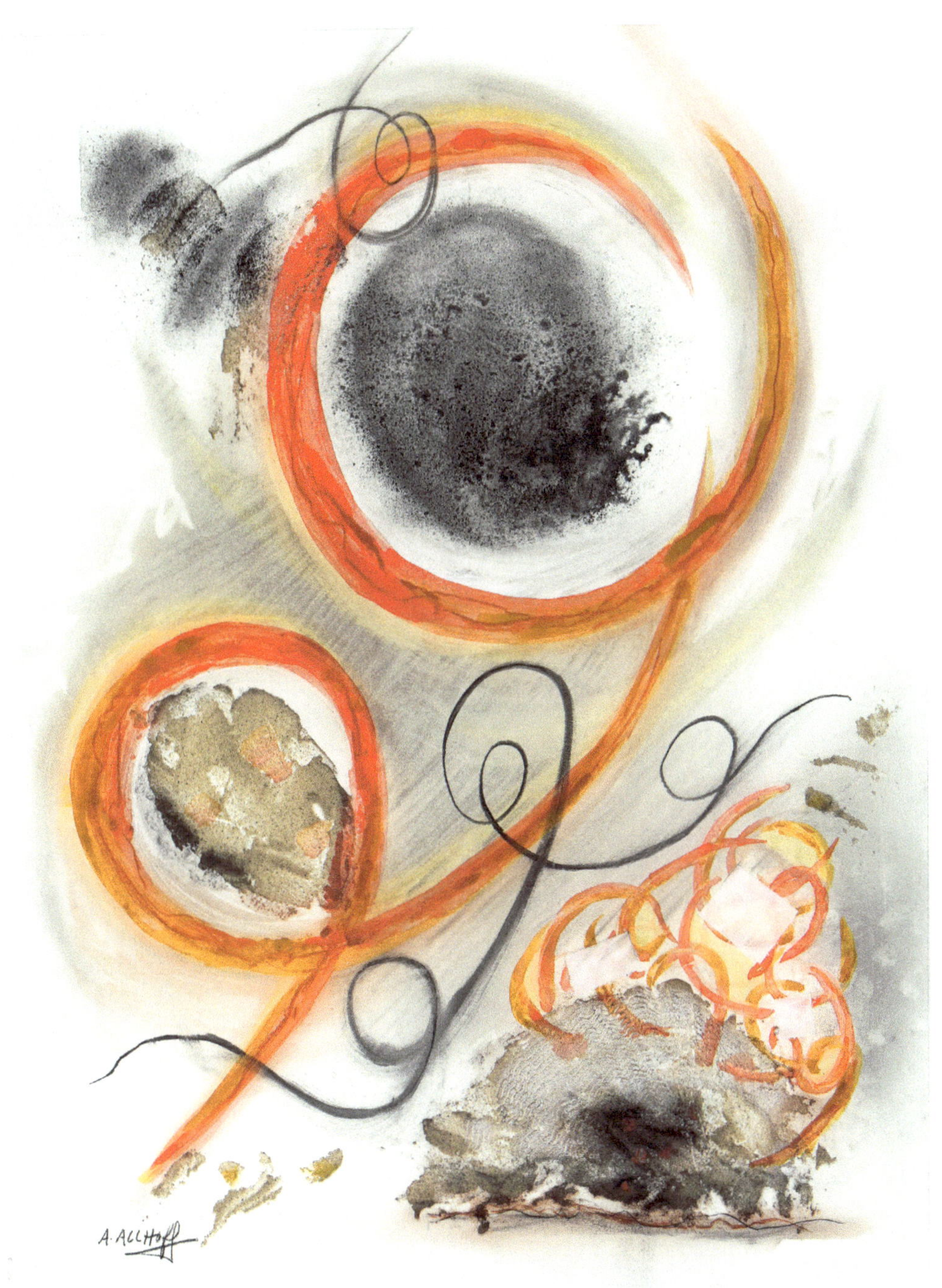

Loop Holes, Alice Allhoff

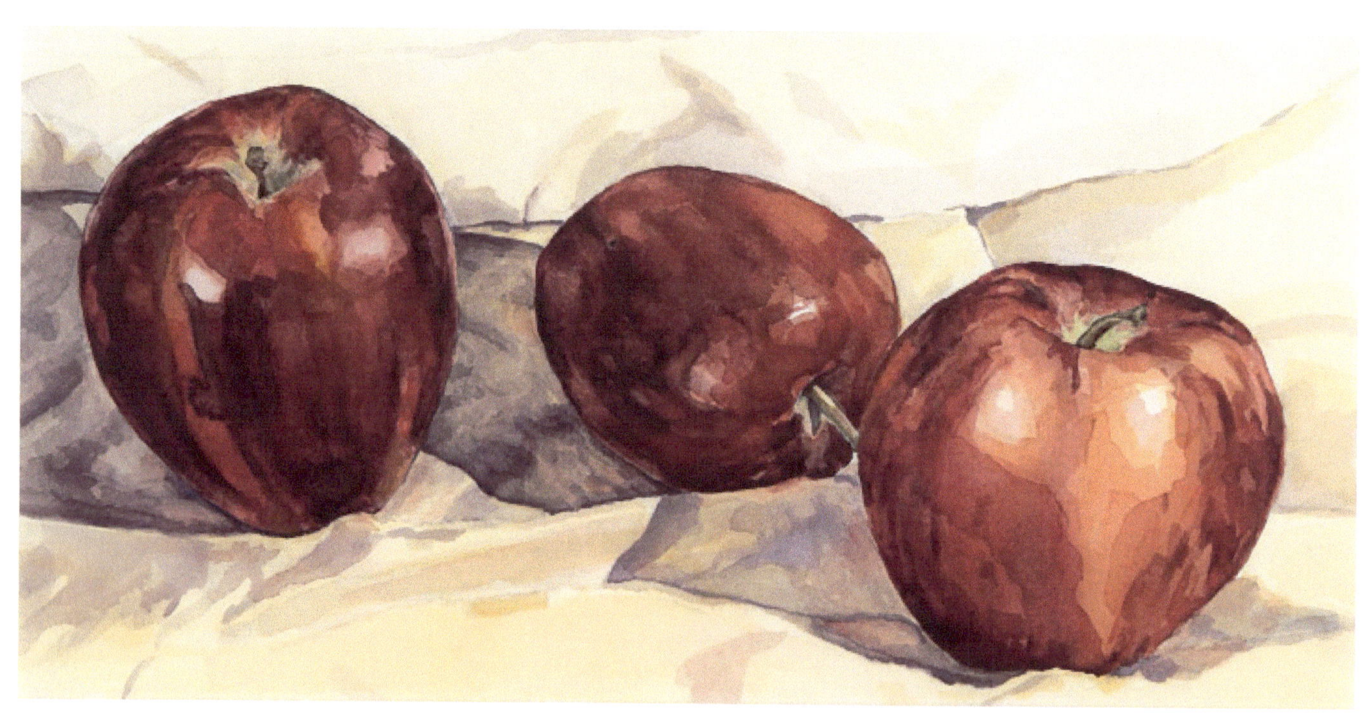

Apples and Shadows, Draea Burnett

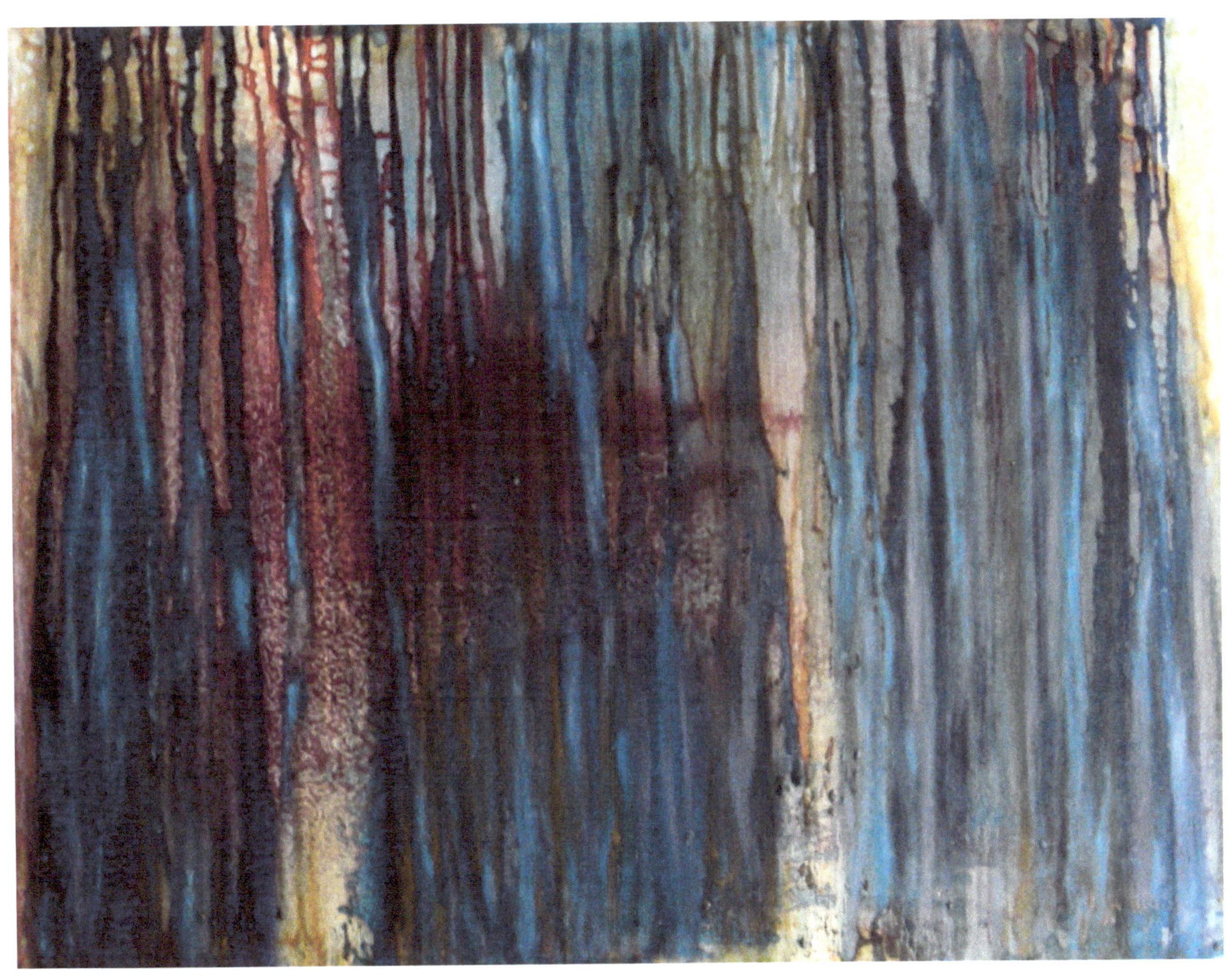

Metro, LaDean Birkhead

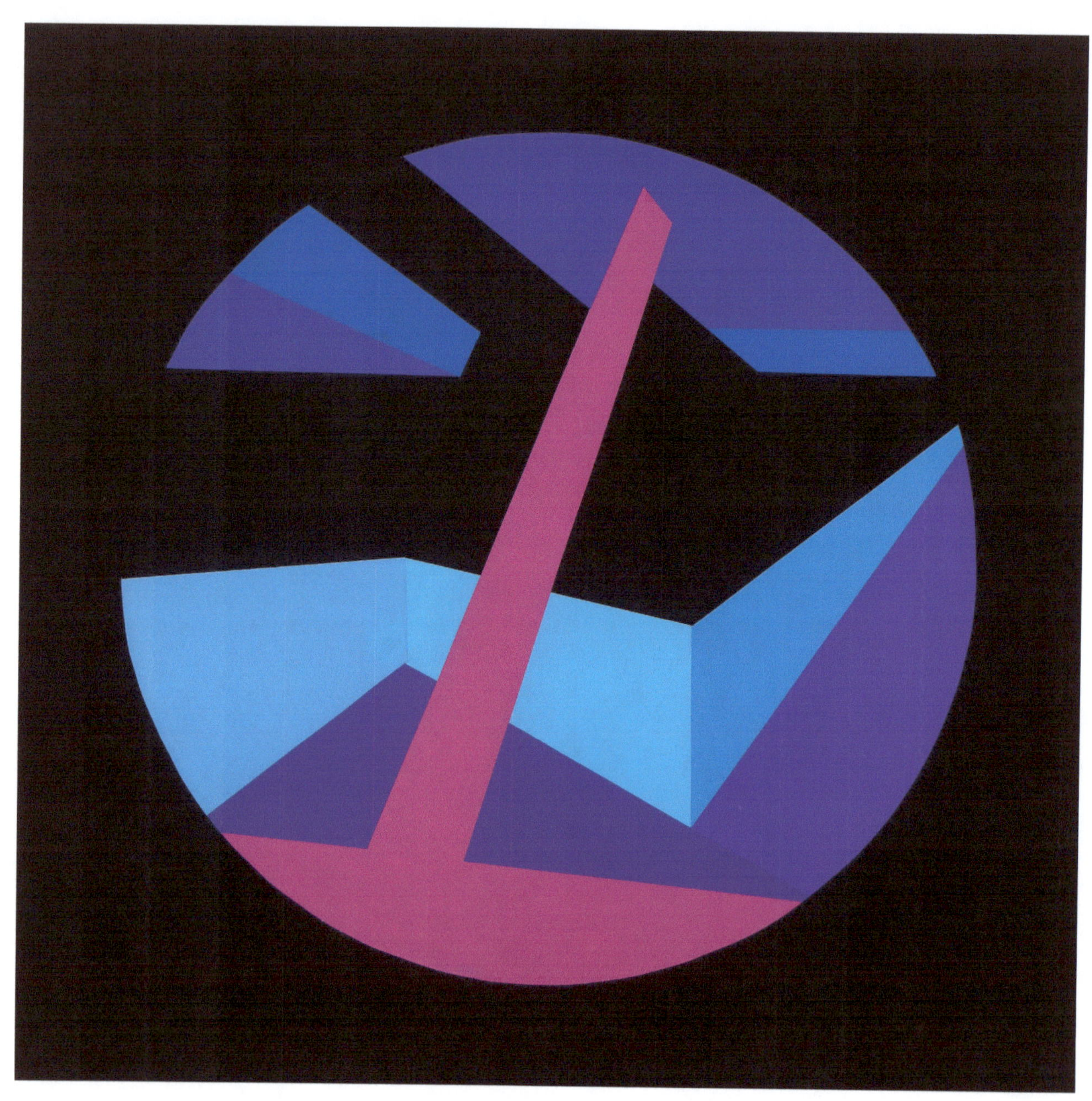

Circle Series II, Jerald Mitchell

spider webs in my hair

Brian Steimel

in the dark of the hot
new summers night
when i am trying to sleep
the spiders are busy in the barn
spinning and weaving fragile webs
to and fro up and down
from doorways and roof beams
from tractor steering wheels to pick axes
creating sticky strings
that get in my hair
the next grey foggy morning

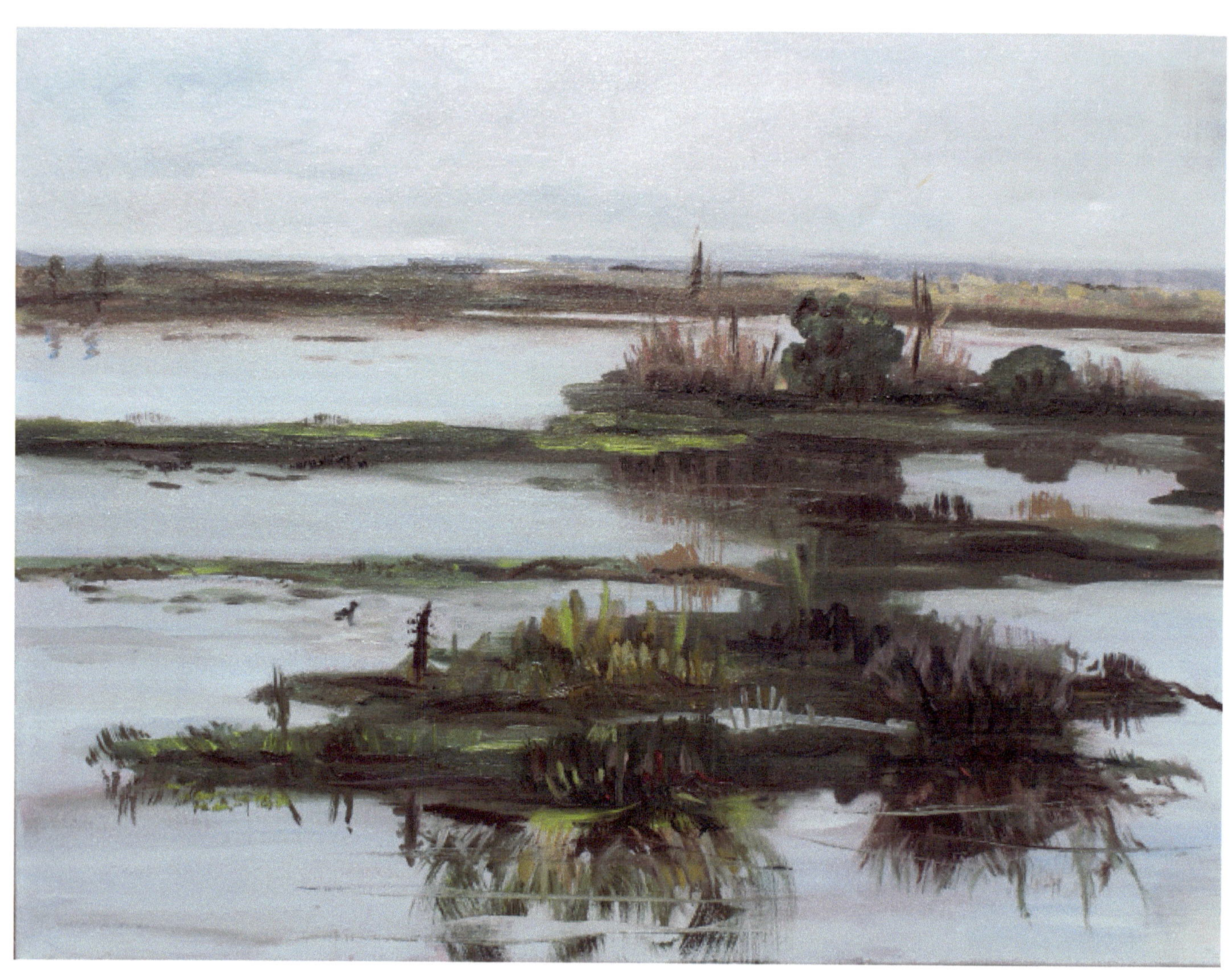

The Marsh, Carol Kery

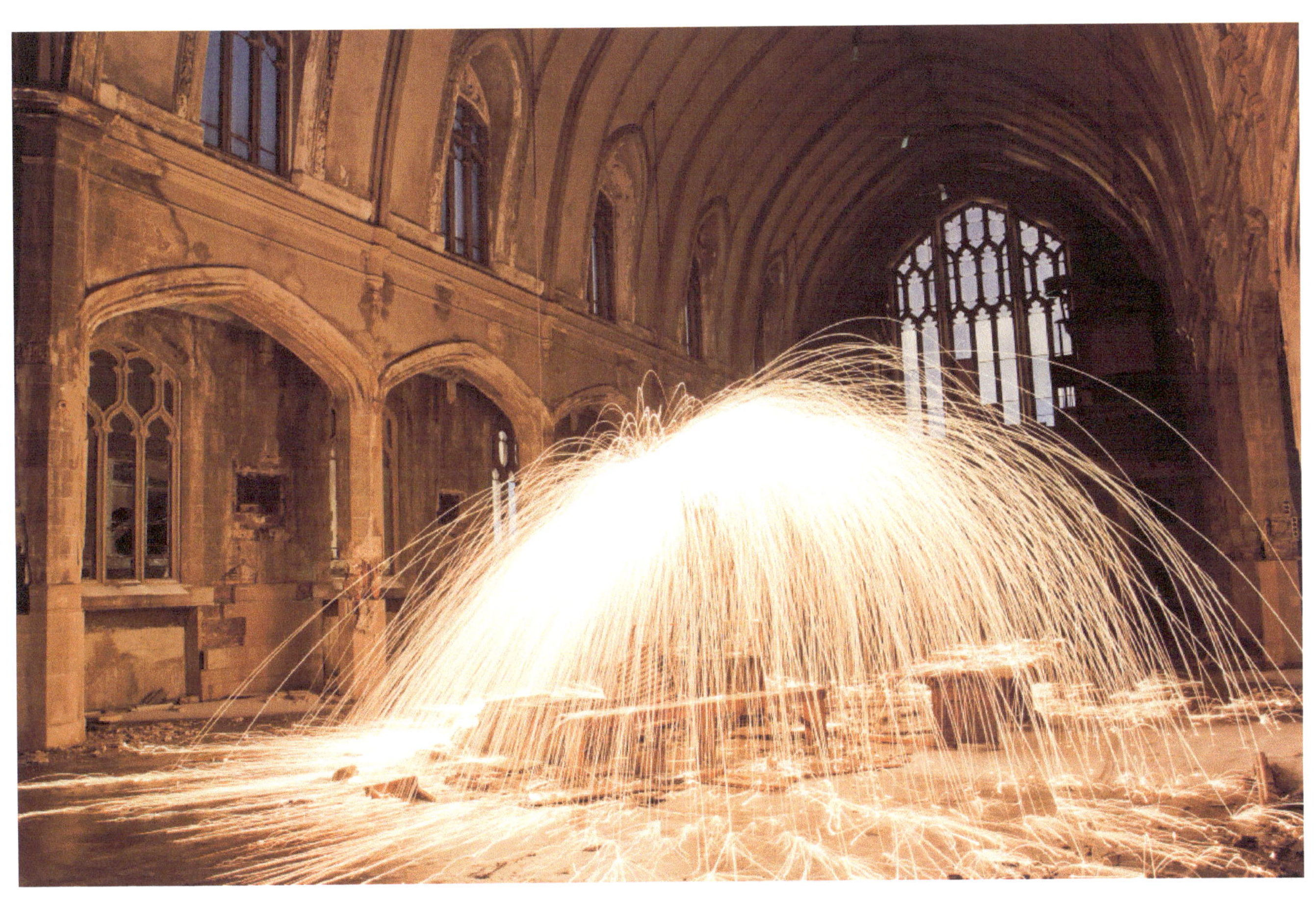

Hephaestus, Vincent Verna

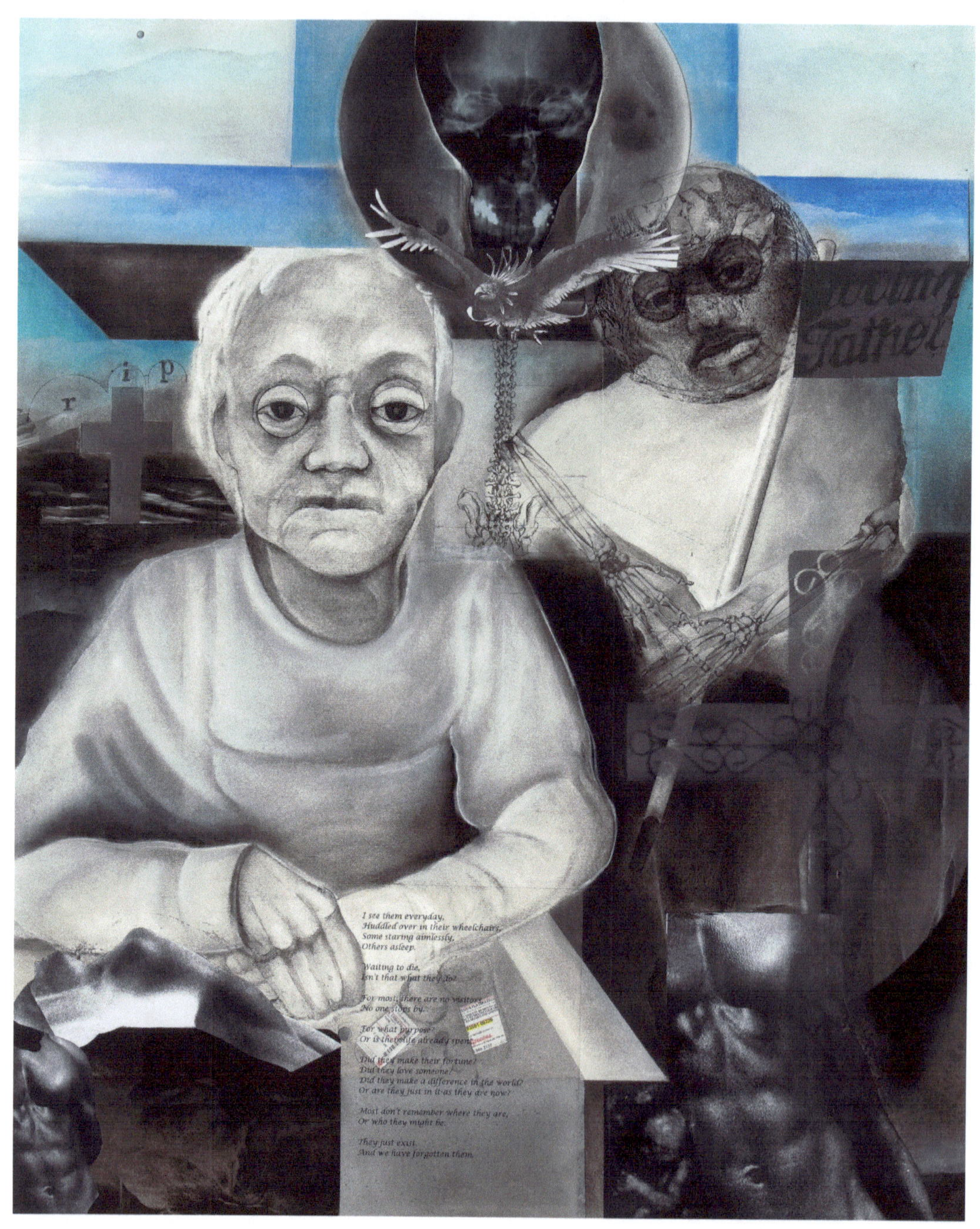

Waiting to Die, Pat Duff

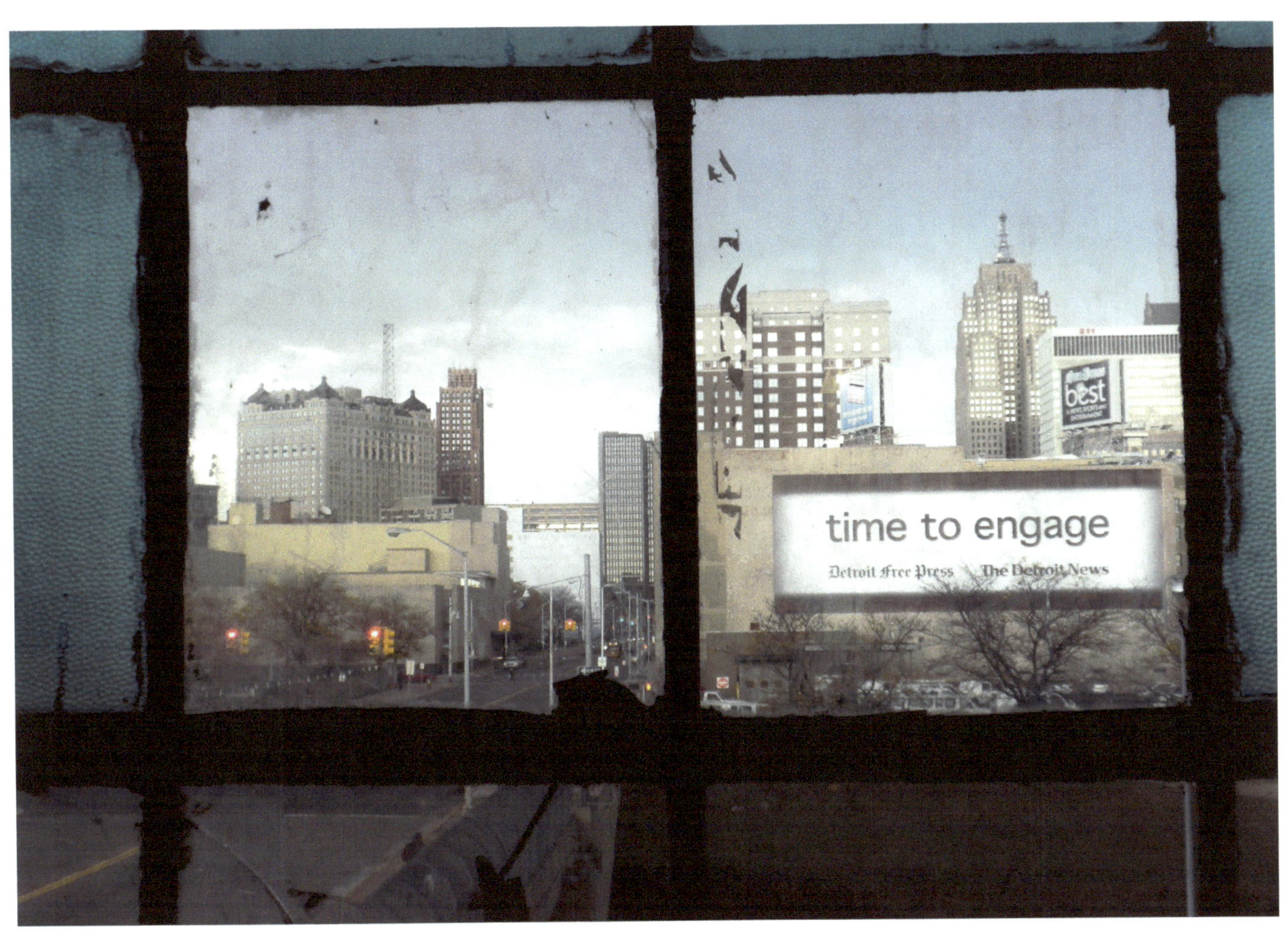

Engage, Lauren Karlisle

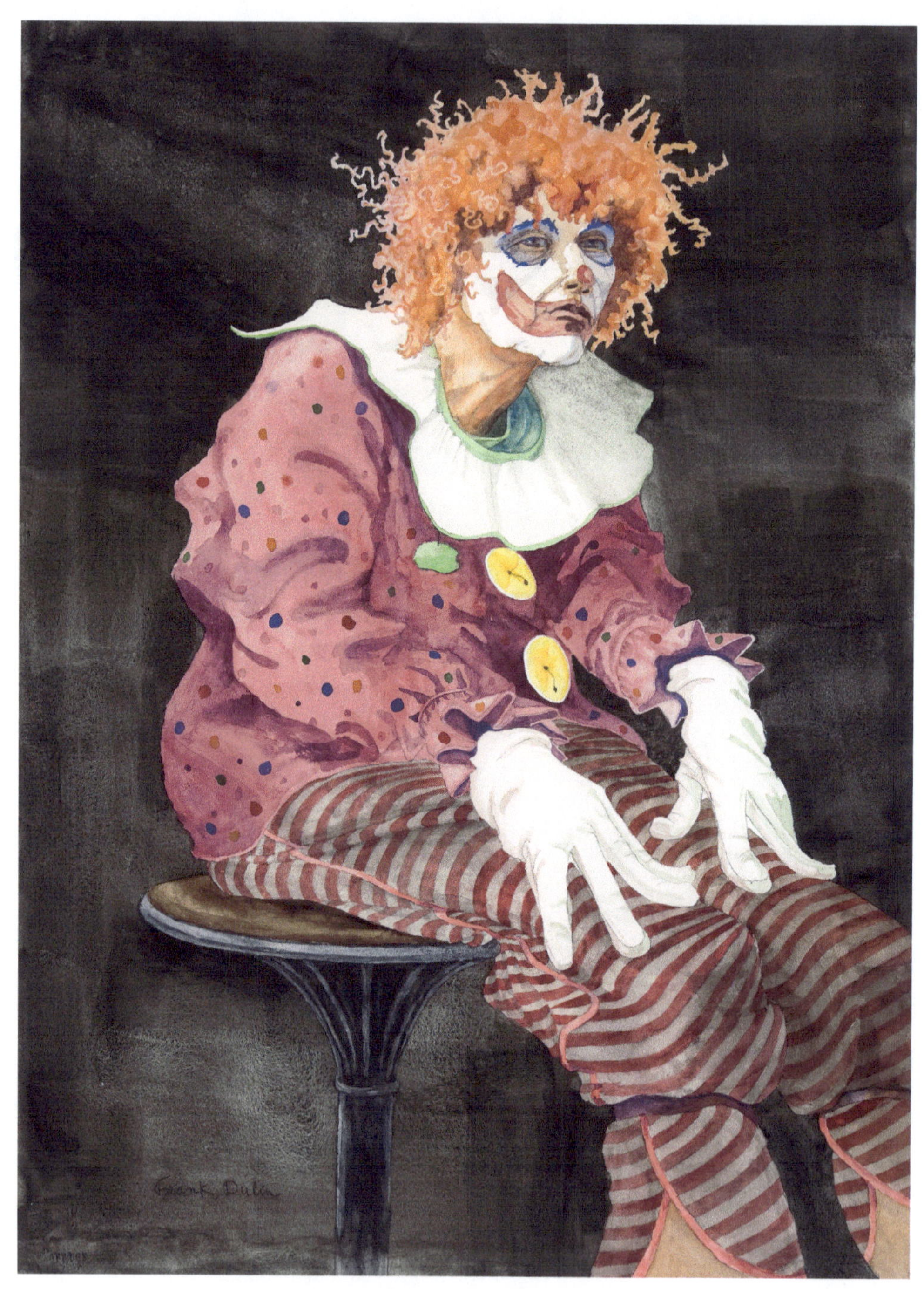

Circus Blues, Frank Dulin

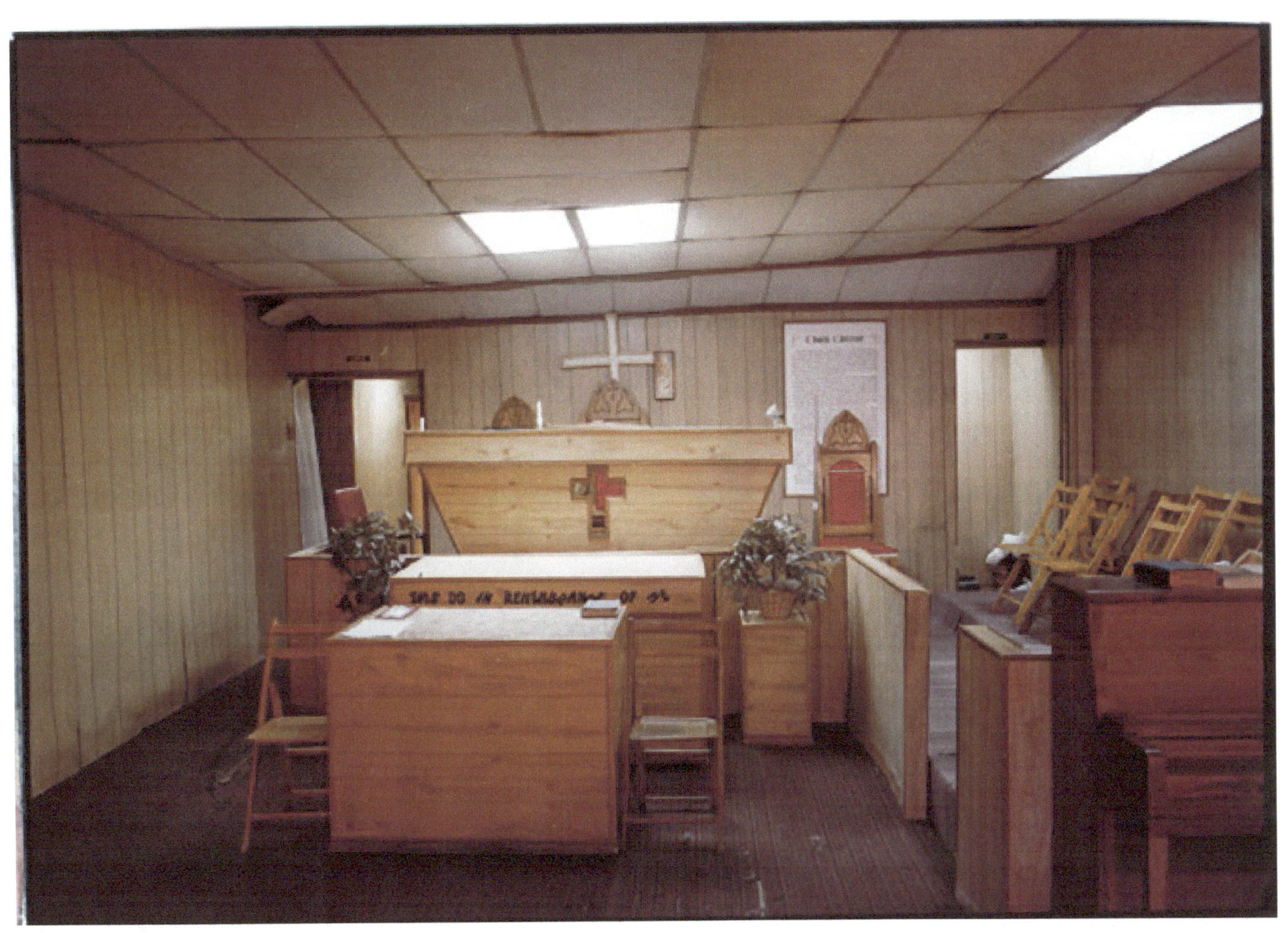

Christ CME Church, Ch Carroll

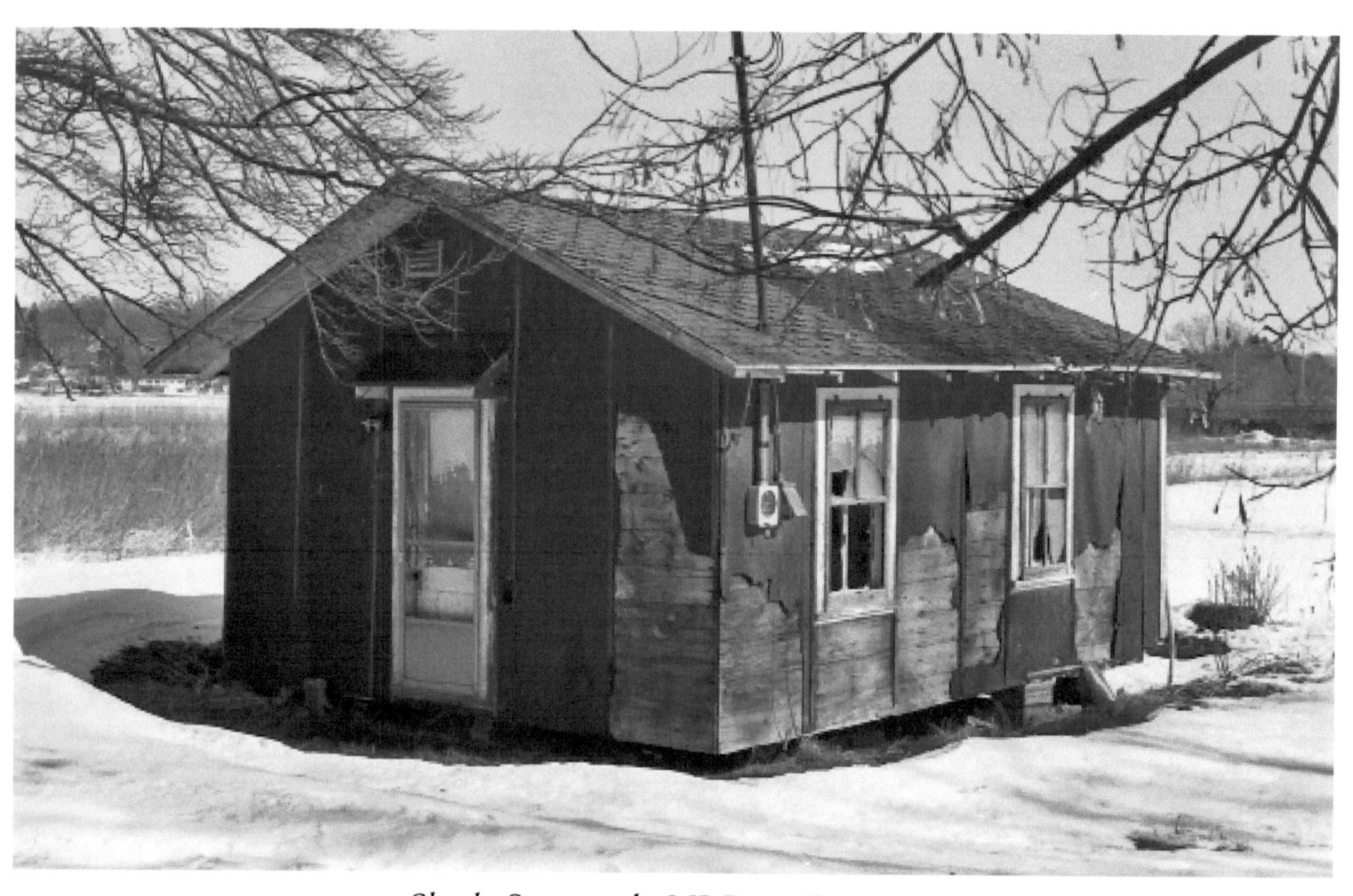

Shack, Saugatauk, MI, Jerry Conway

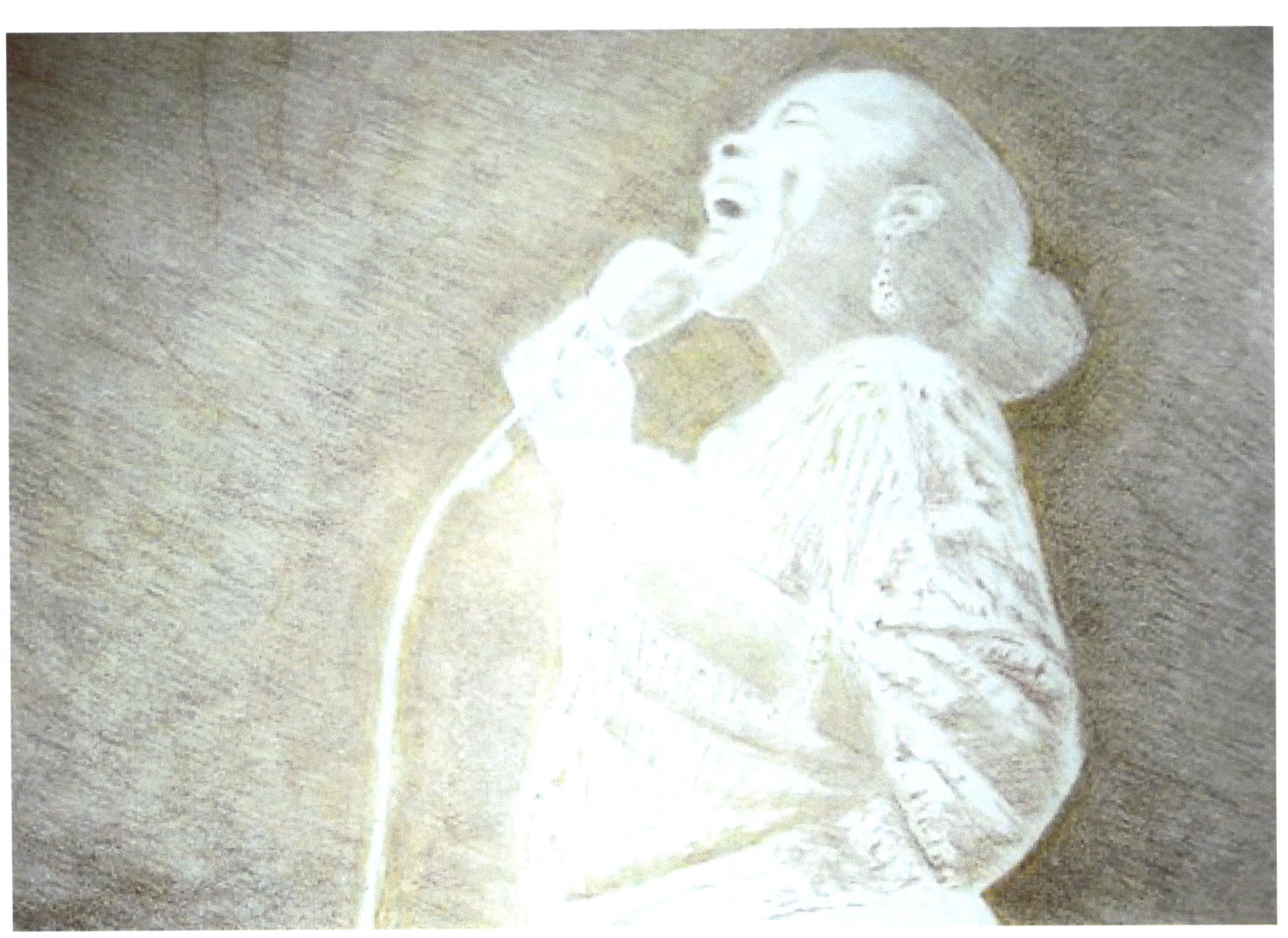

Betty Carter, Charles Ezra Ferrell

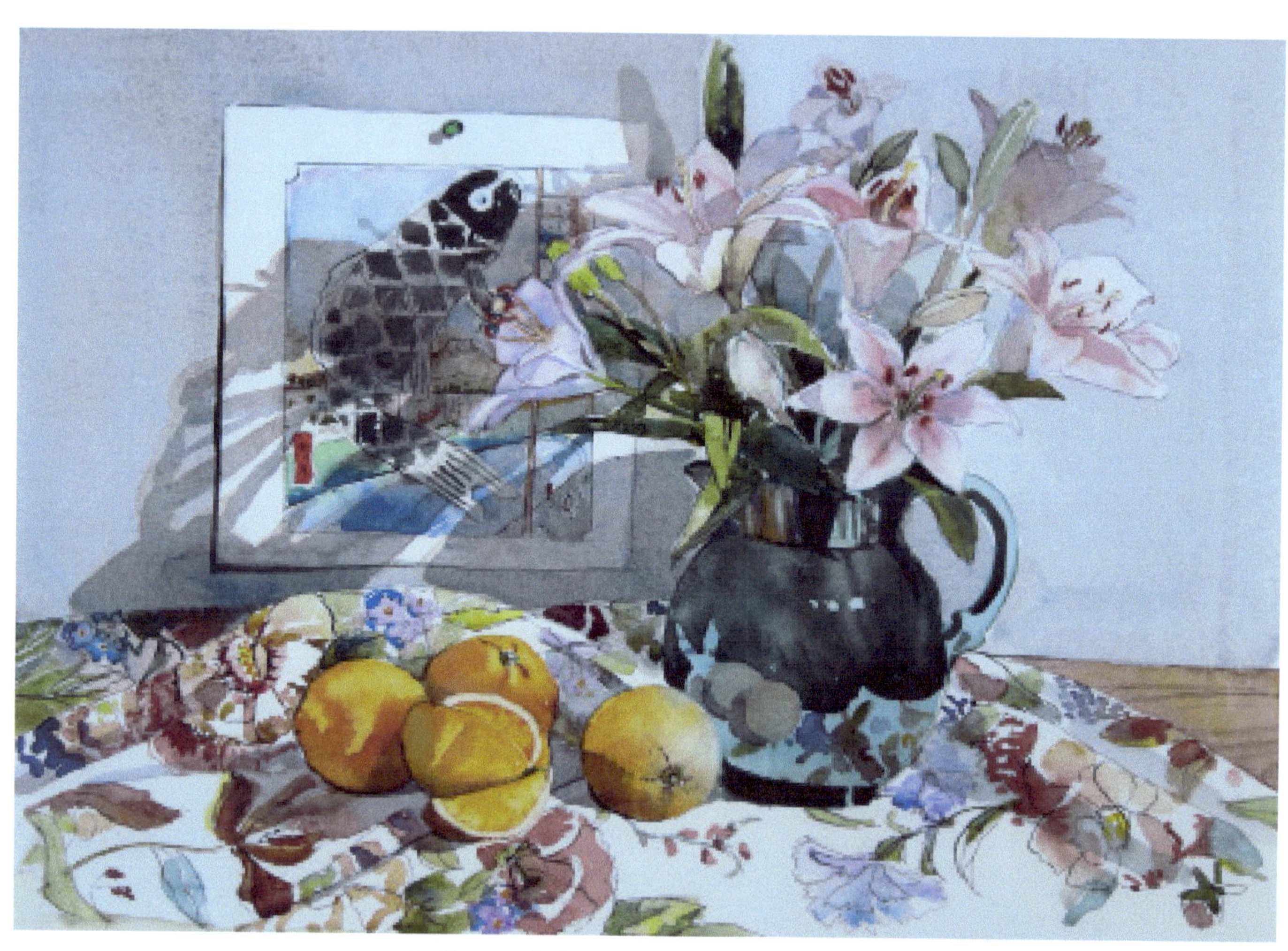

Lillies and Oranges, Eugenia Hoag

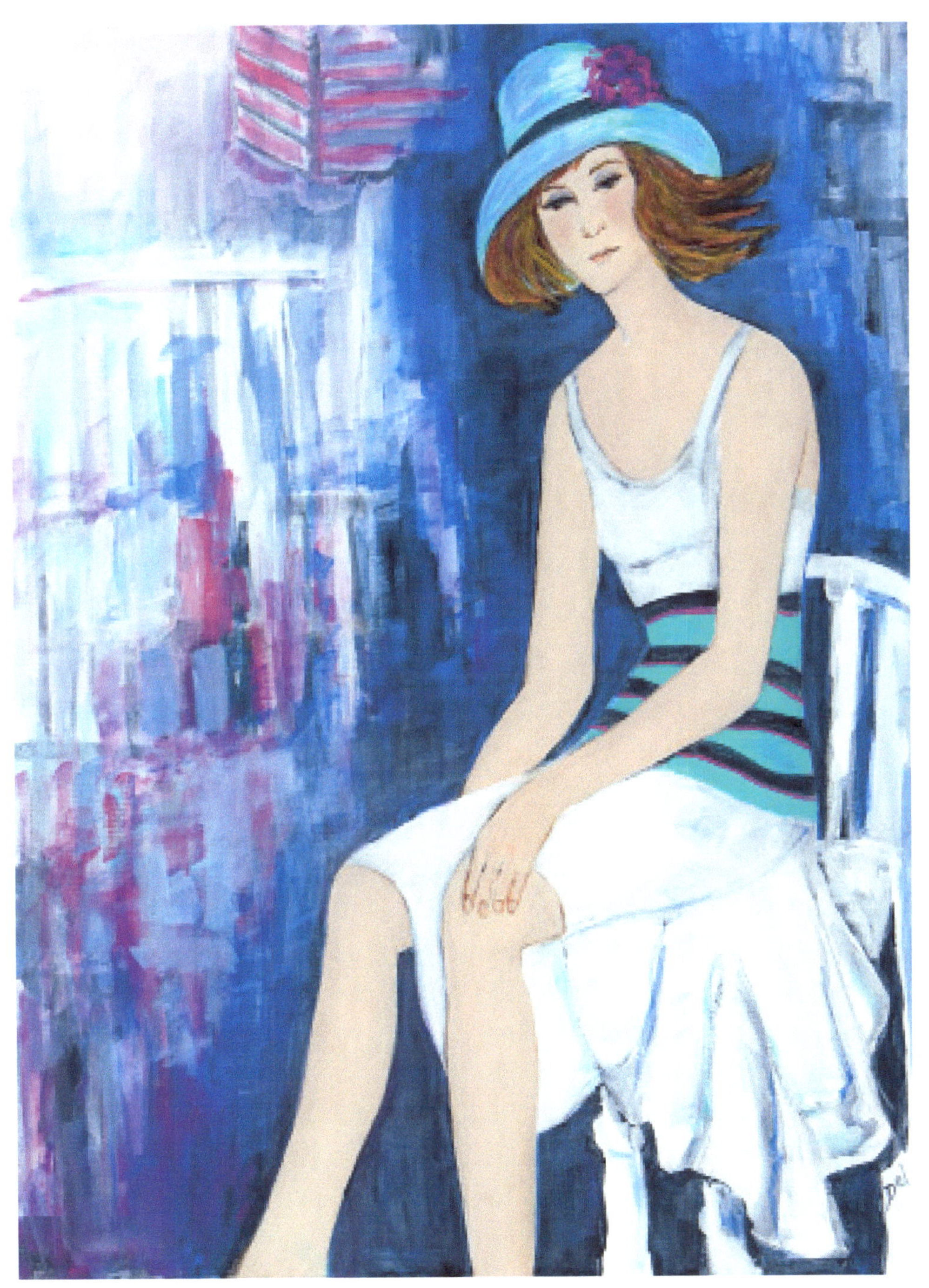

Reflections, Delphine Iwankowski

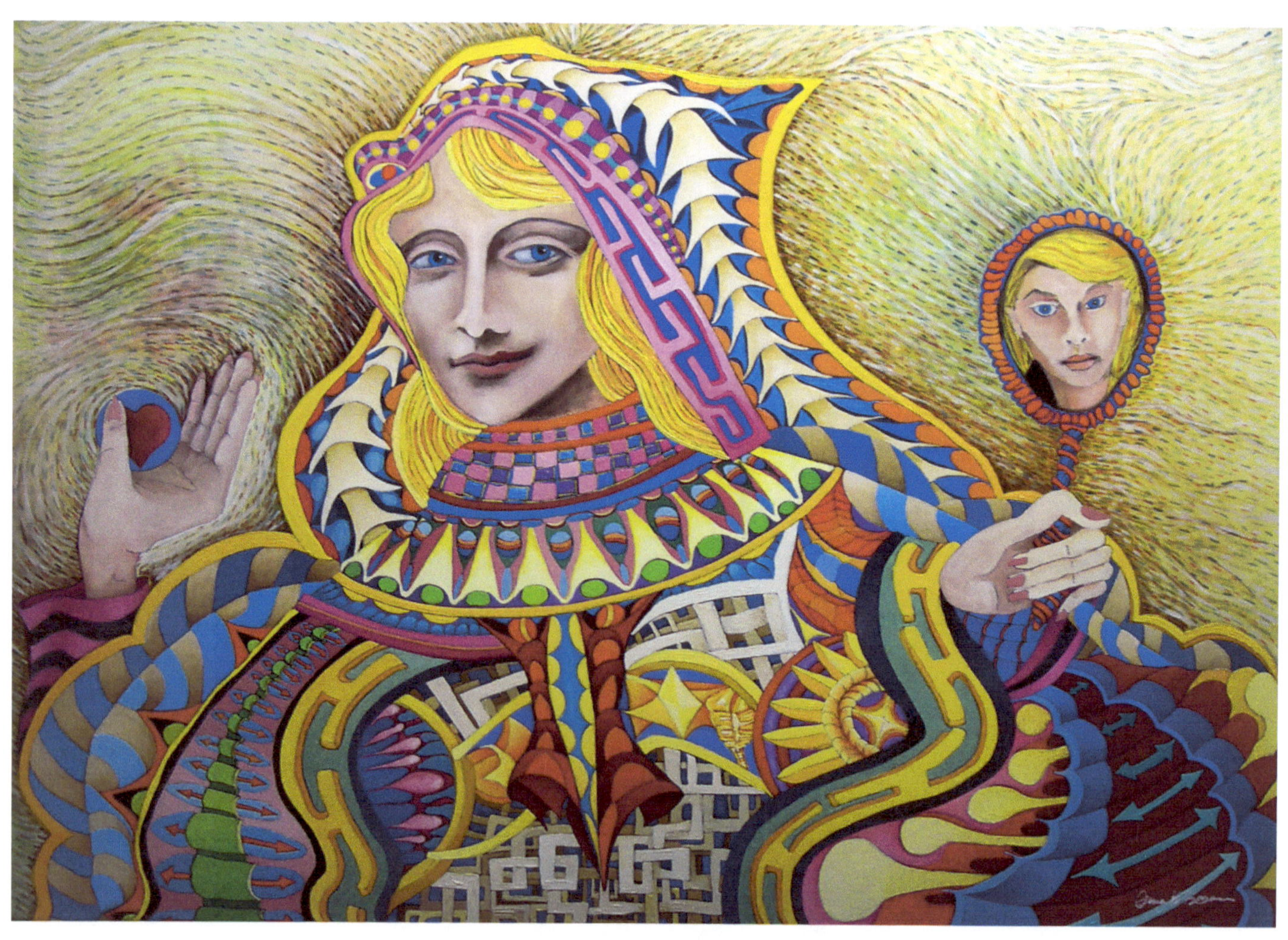

Queen of Hearts, James Homer Brown

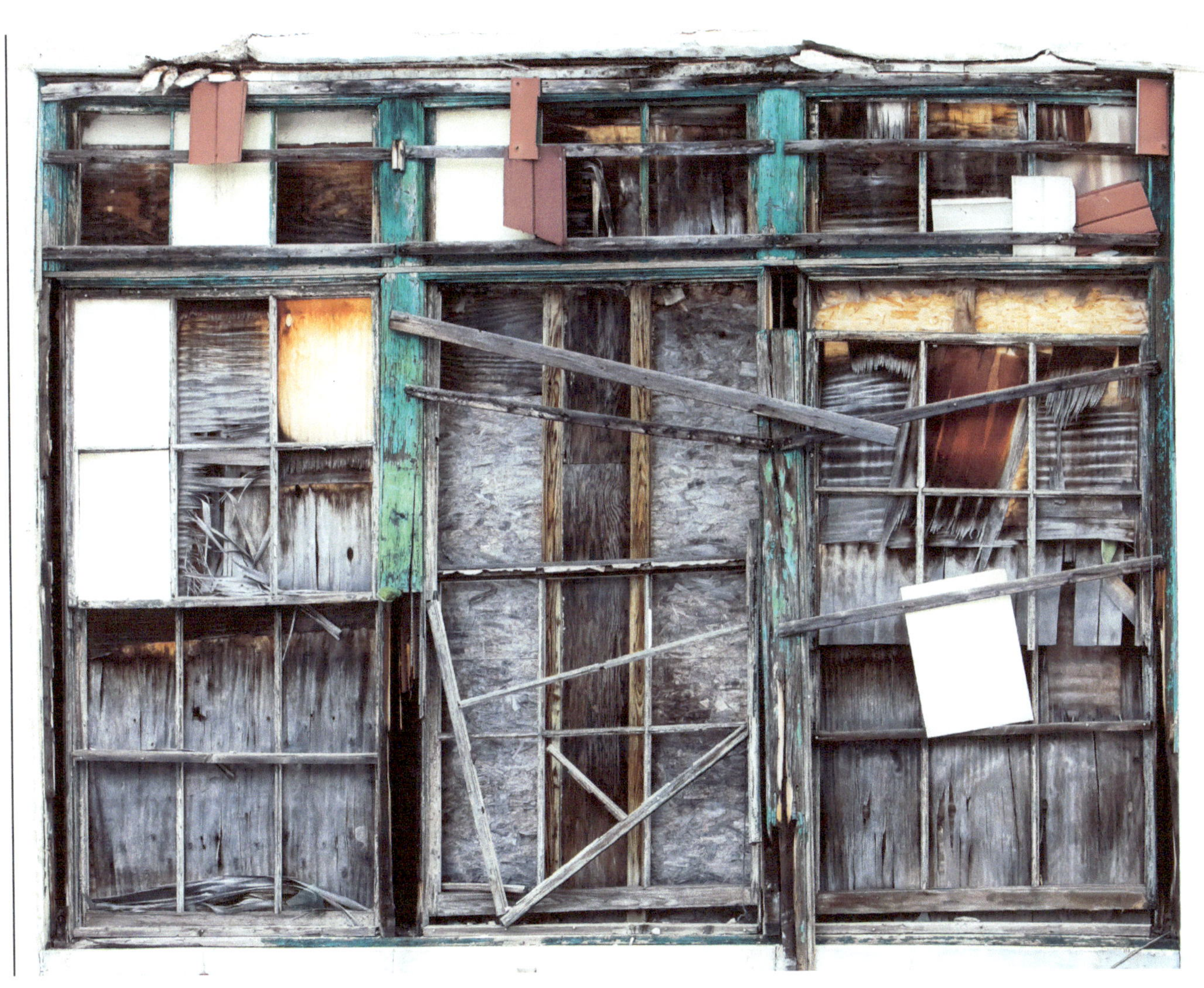

Material World III, Beverly Benson Wolf

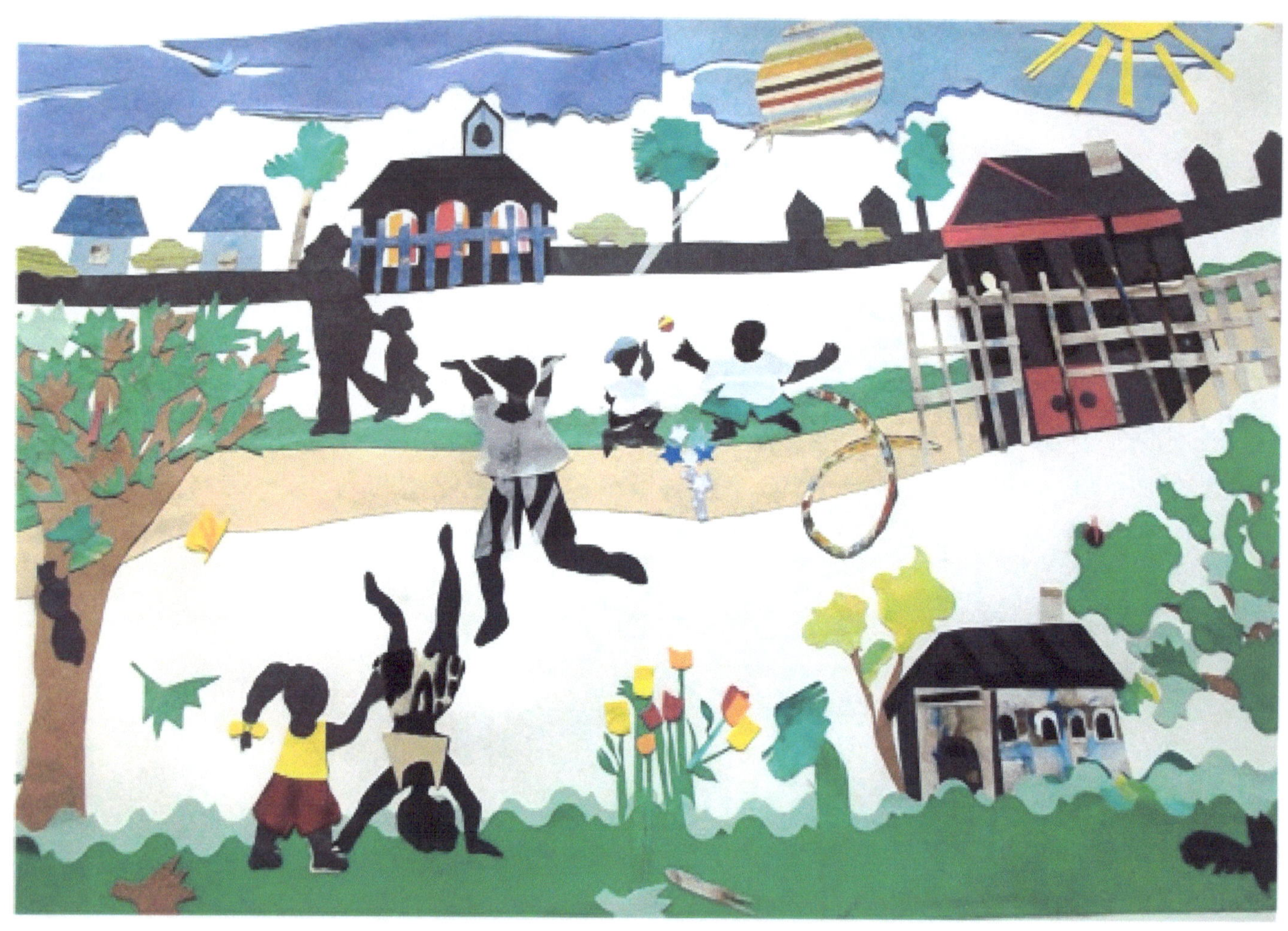

Fun Things II, Adwoa Muwzea

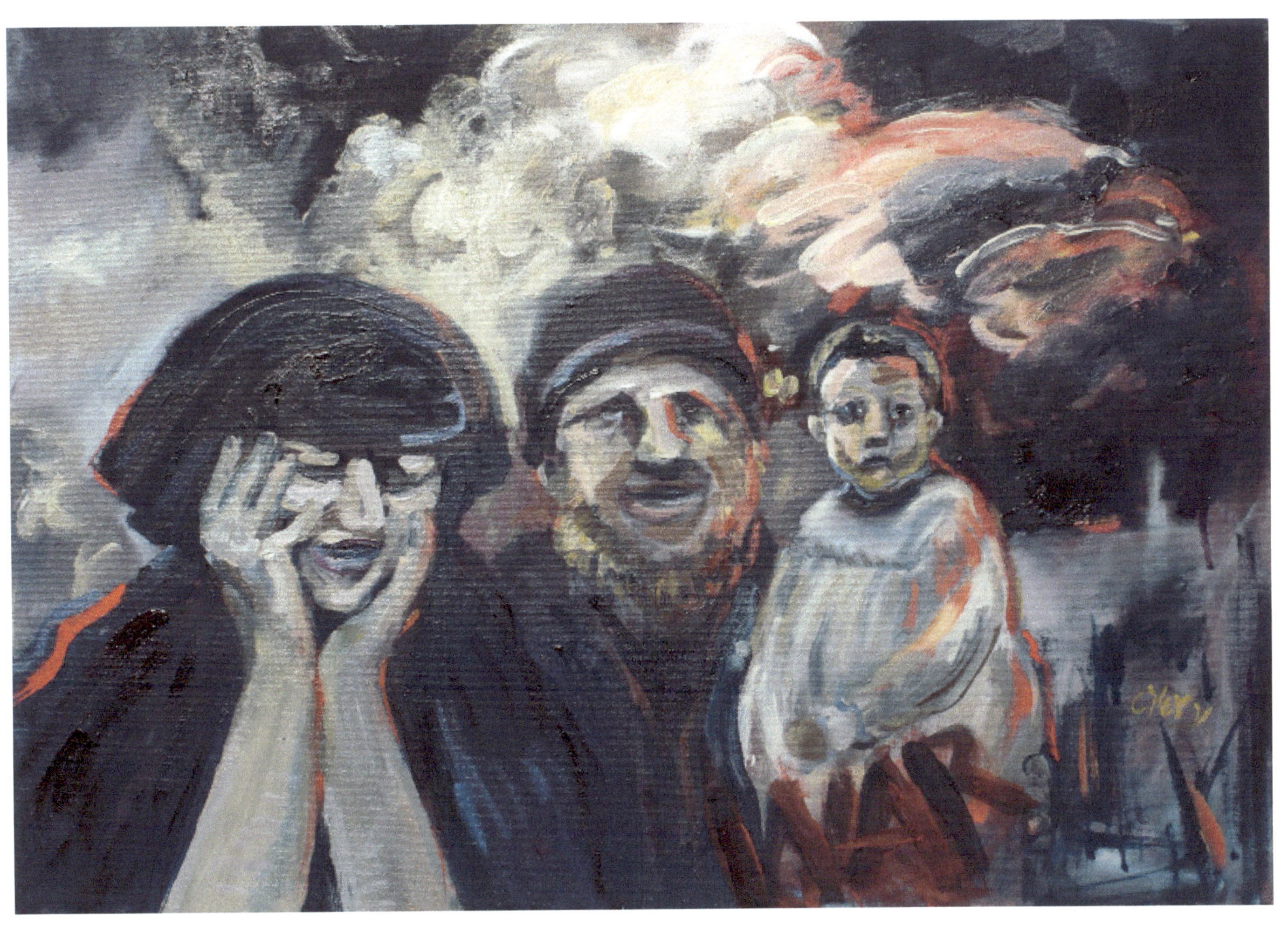

War, Carol Kery

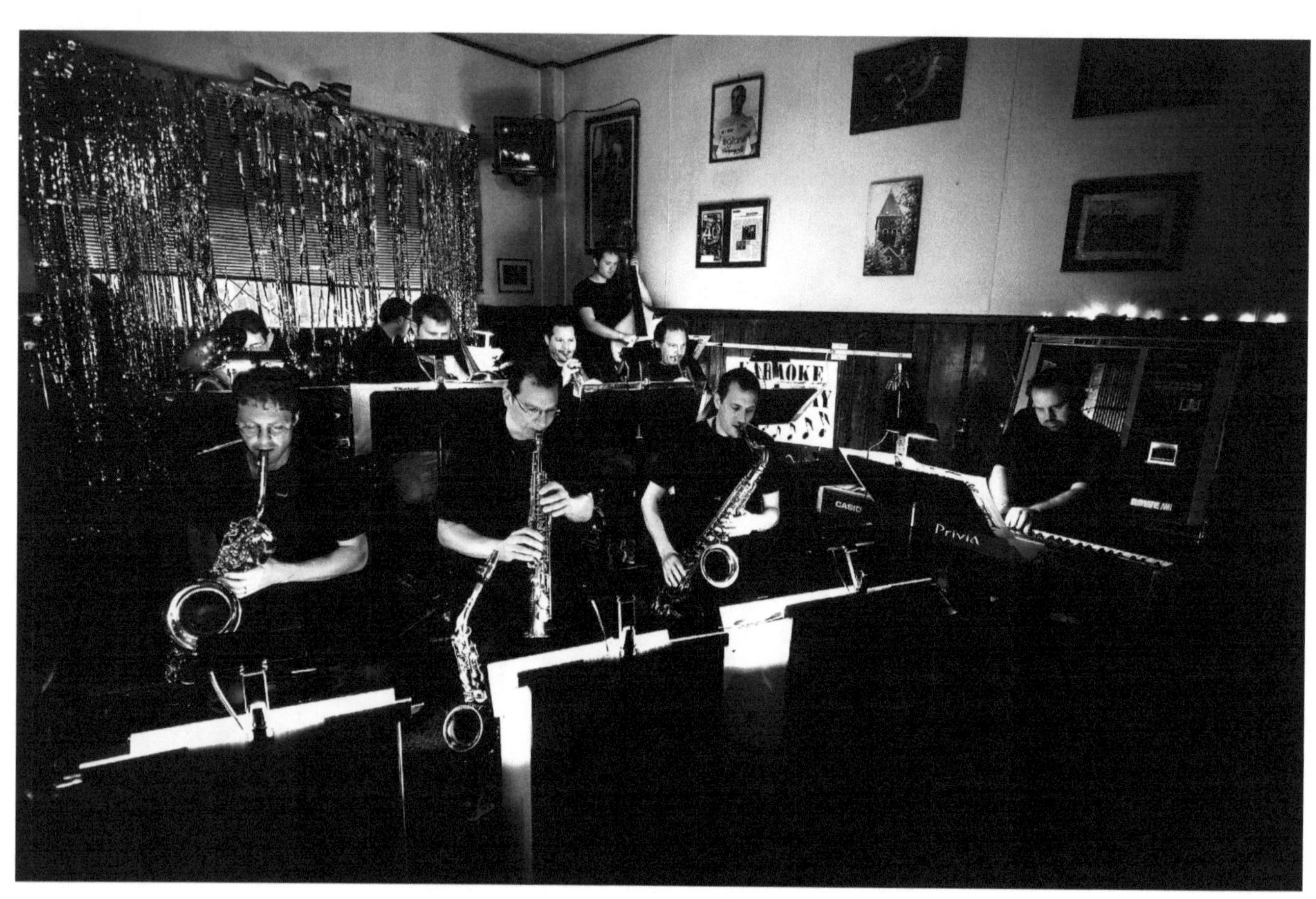

How Much Big Band Can You, Terri Light

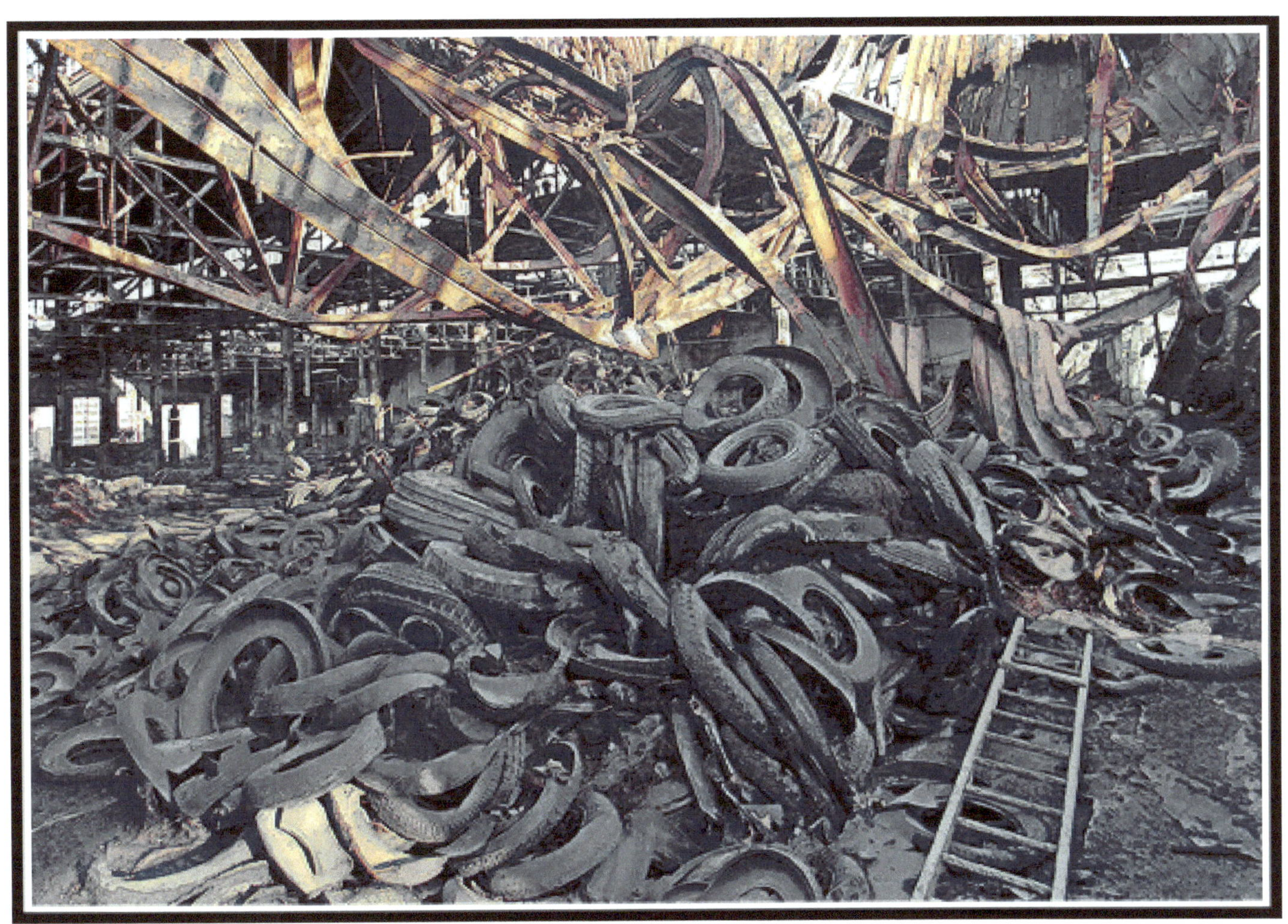

After the Fire #3, Donna Cyrbok

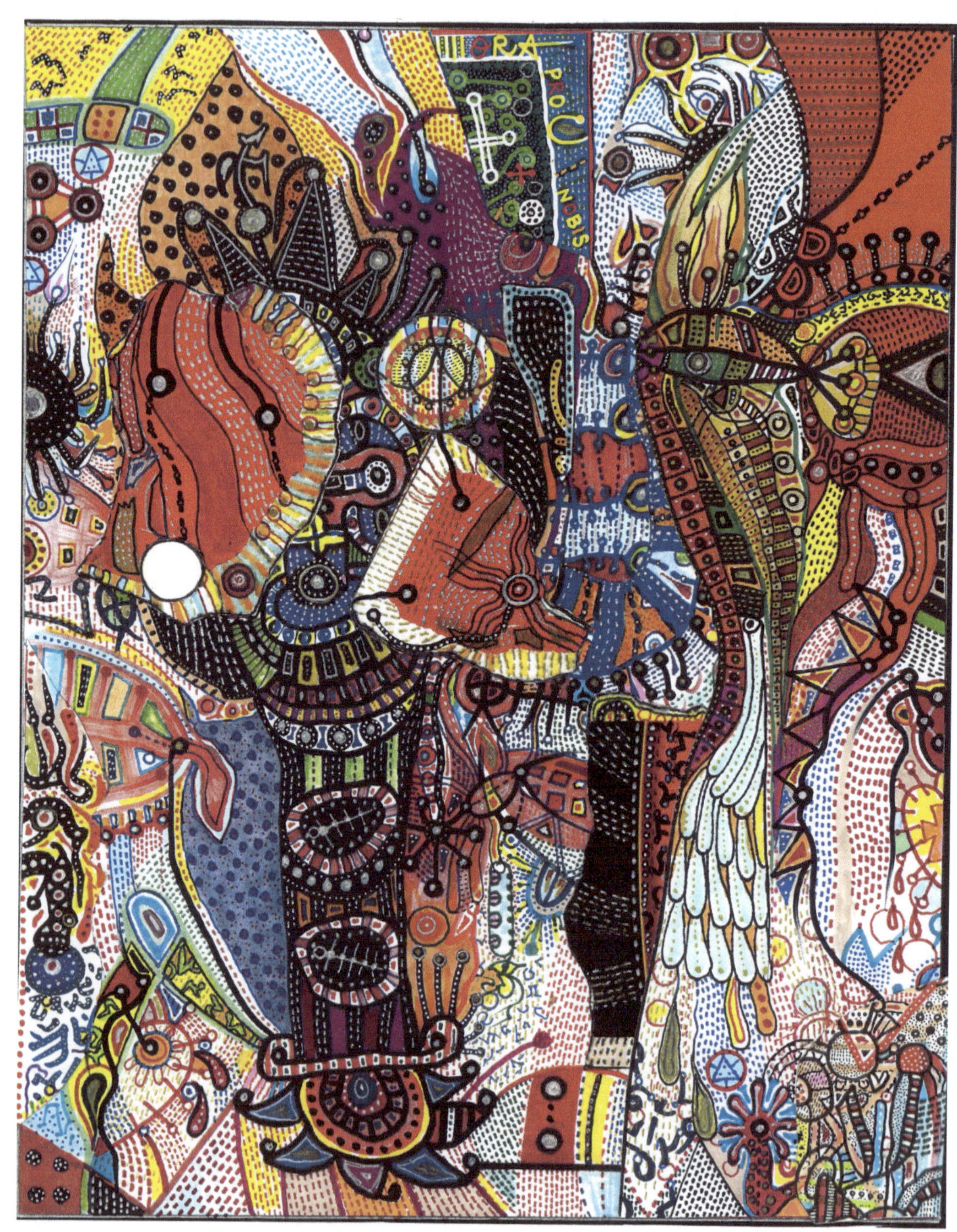

Maskeraider, Charles Alexander

FLEXIBILITY

Ellen Hildreth

Like a straight tall pine
Like a limber lombardy
Like a supple tan terrier
Stretching 'til her body should break
In the noonday life saving sun
A butterfly on the fence
Bends over backwards
Sighing, "Welcome to California"

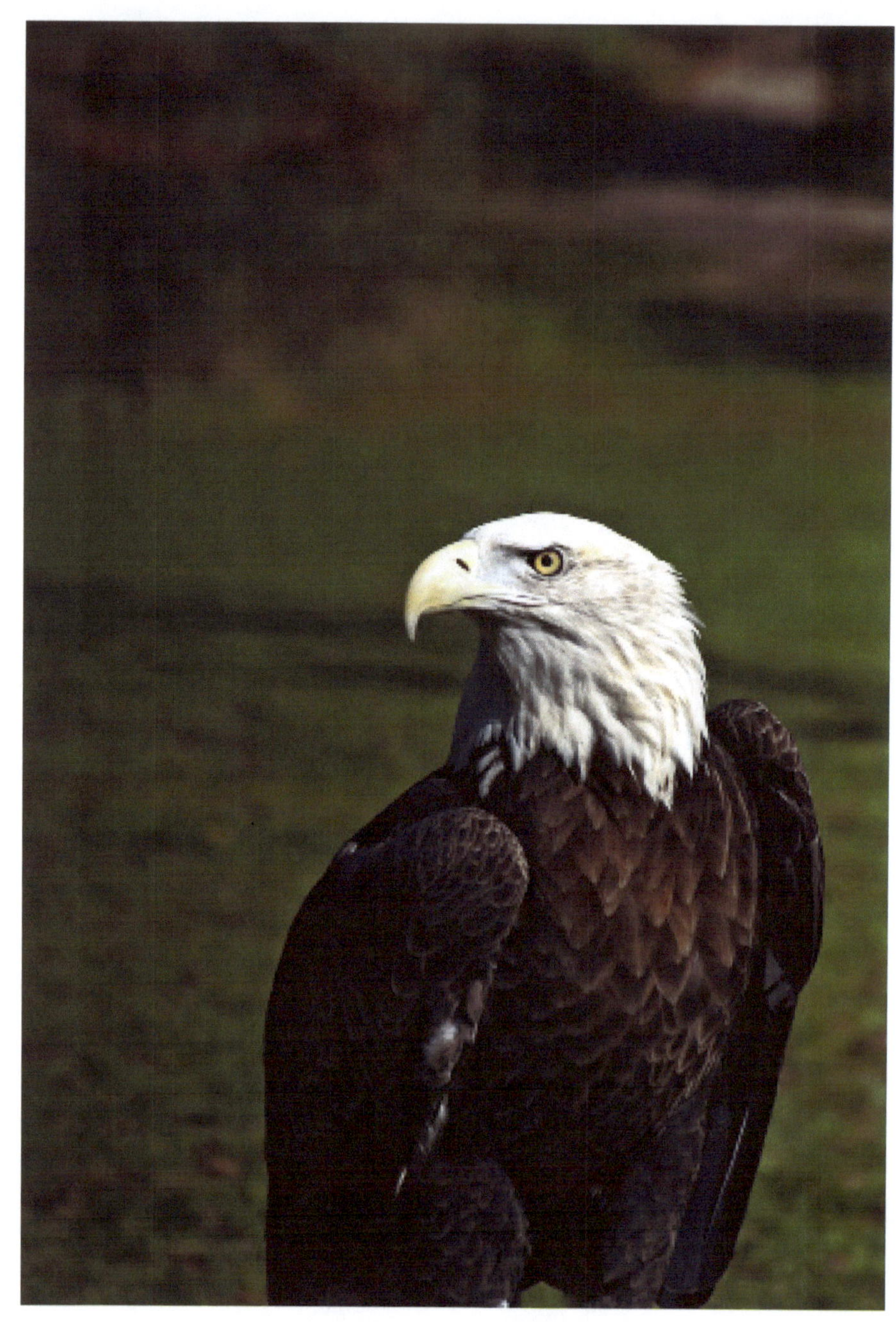

Great Bald Eagle, Nelson Pont

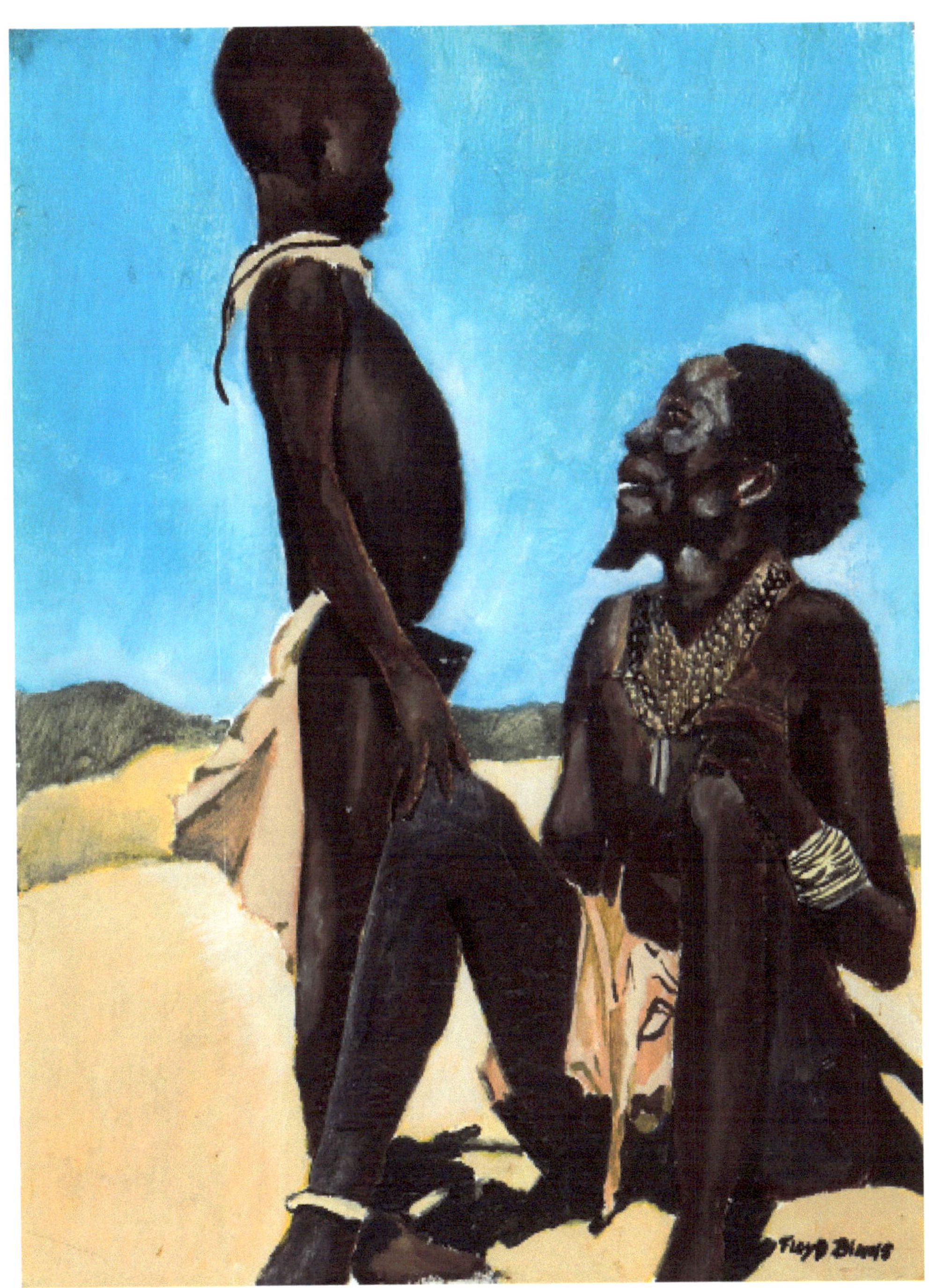

Lesson Learned, Floyd Binns

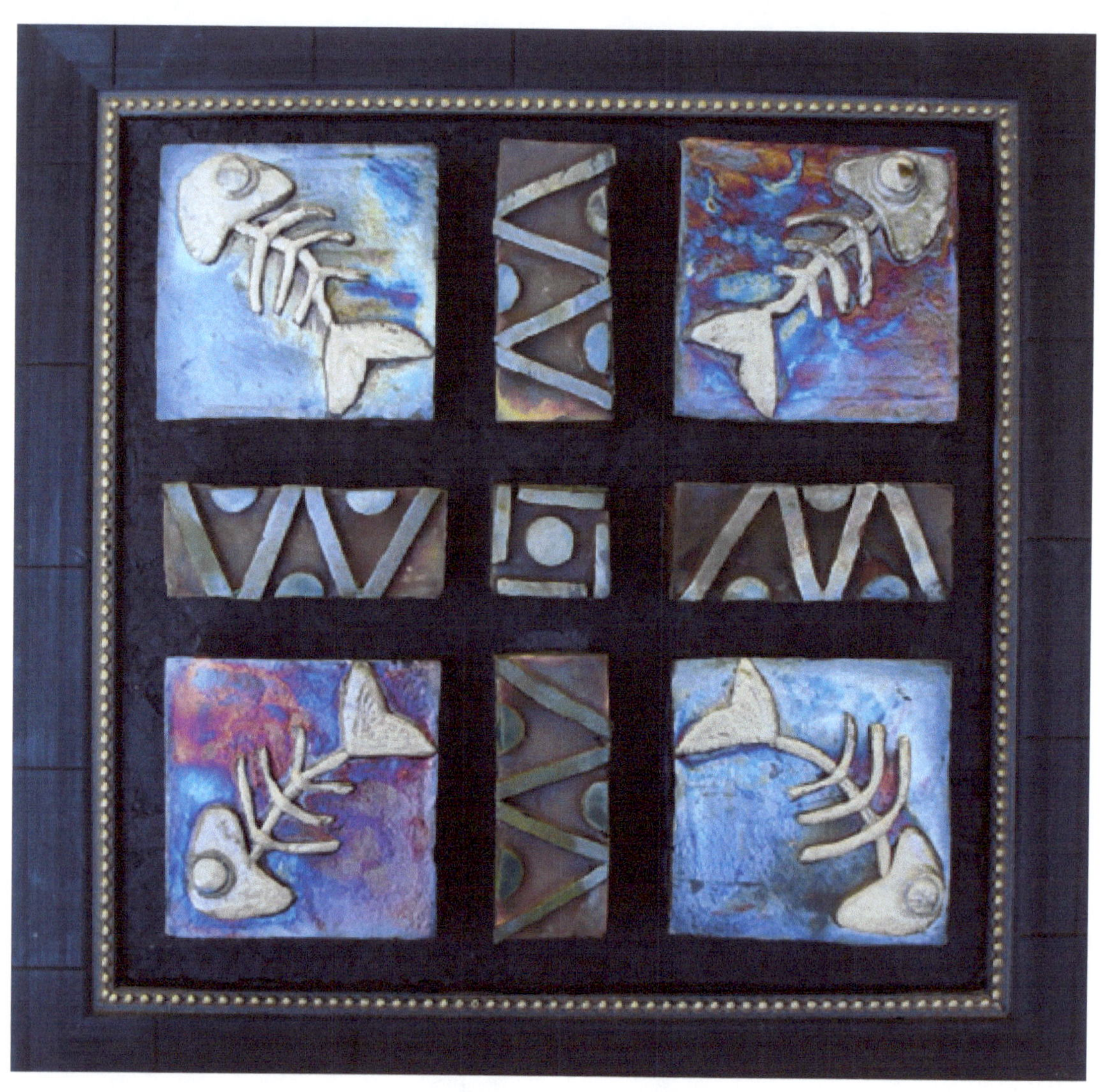

Untitled, Amy Wolfe

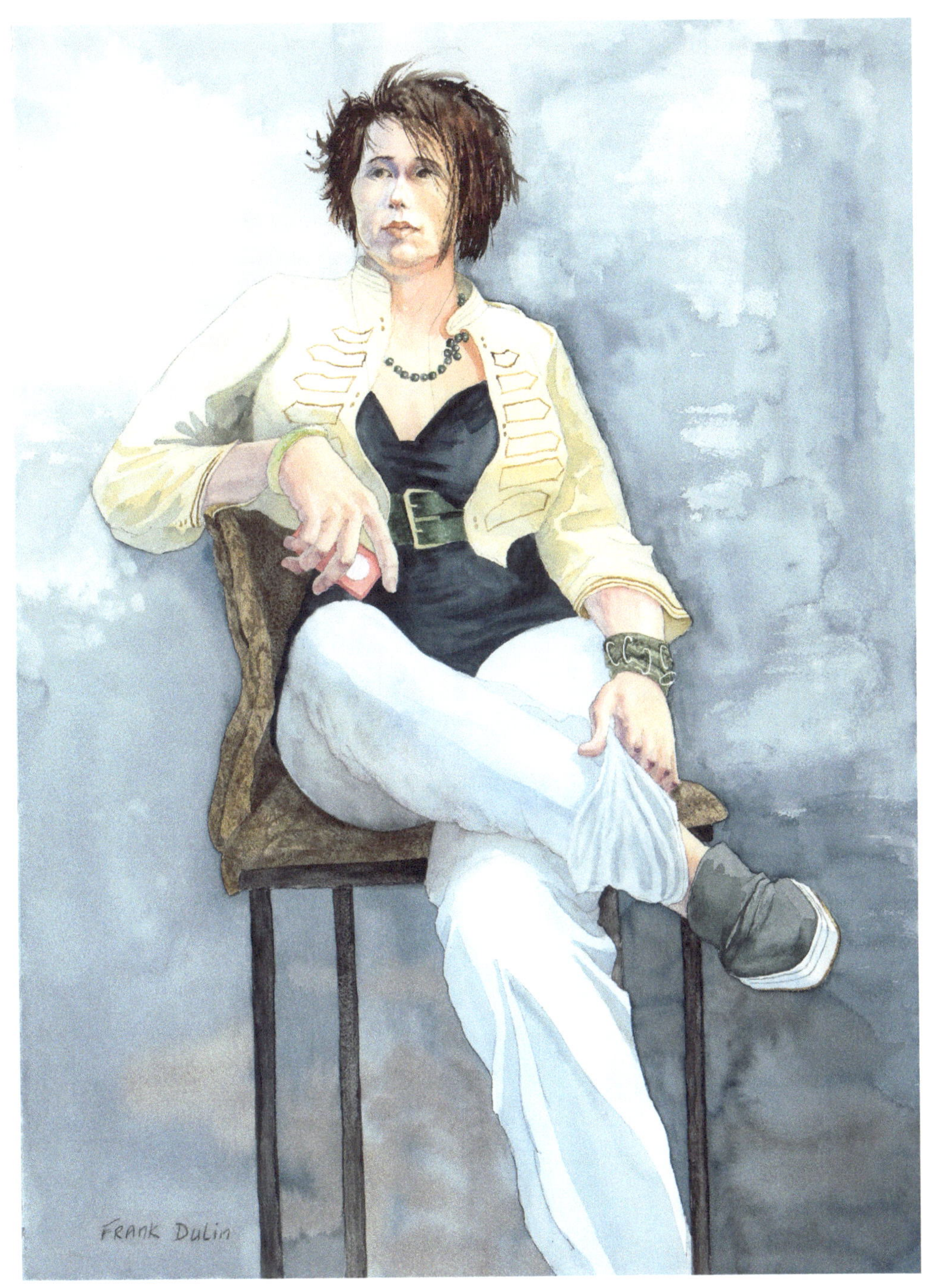

Cassie, Frank Dulin

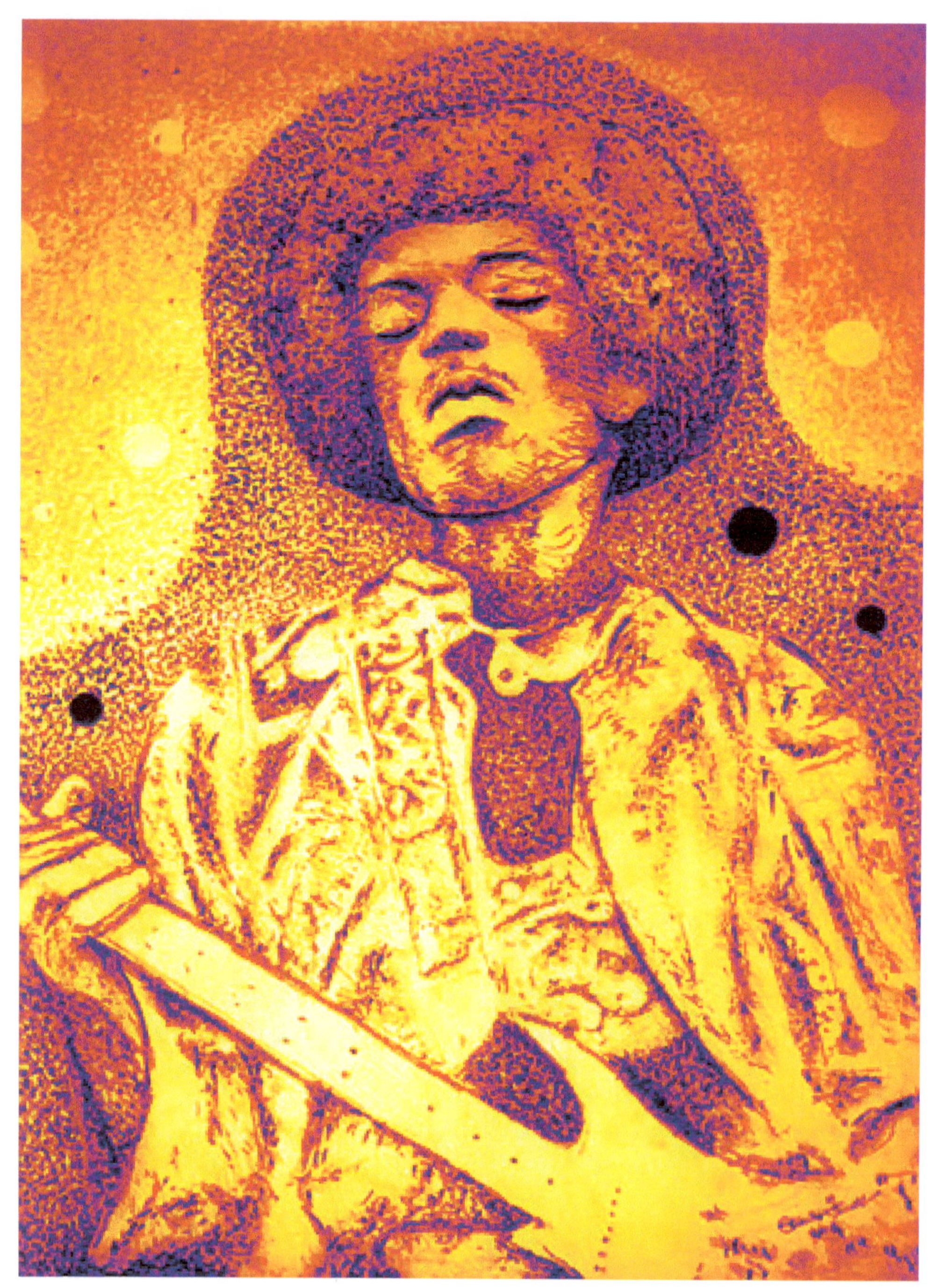

Jimi - Machine Gun, Charles Ezra Ferrell

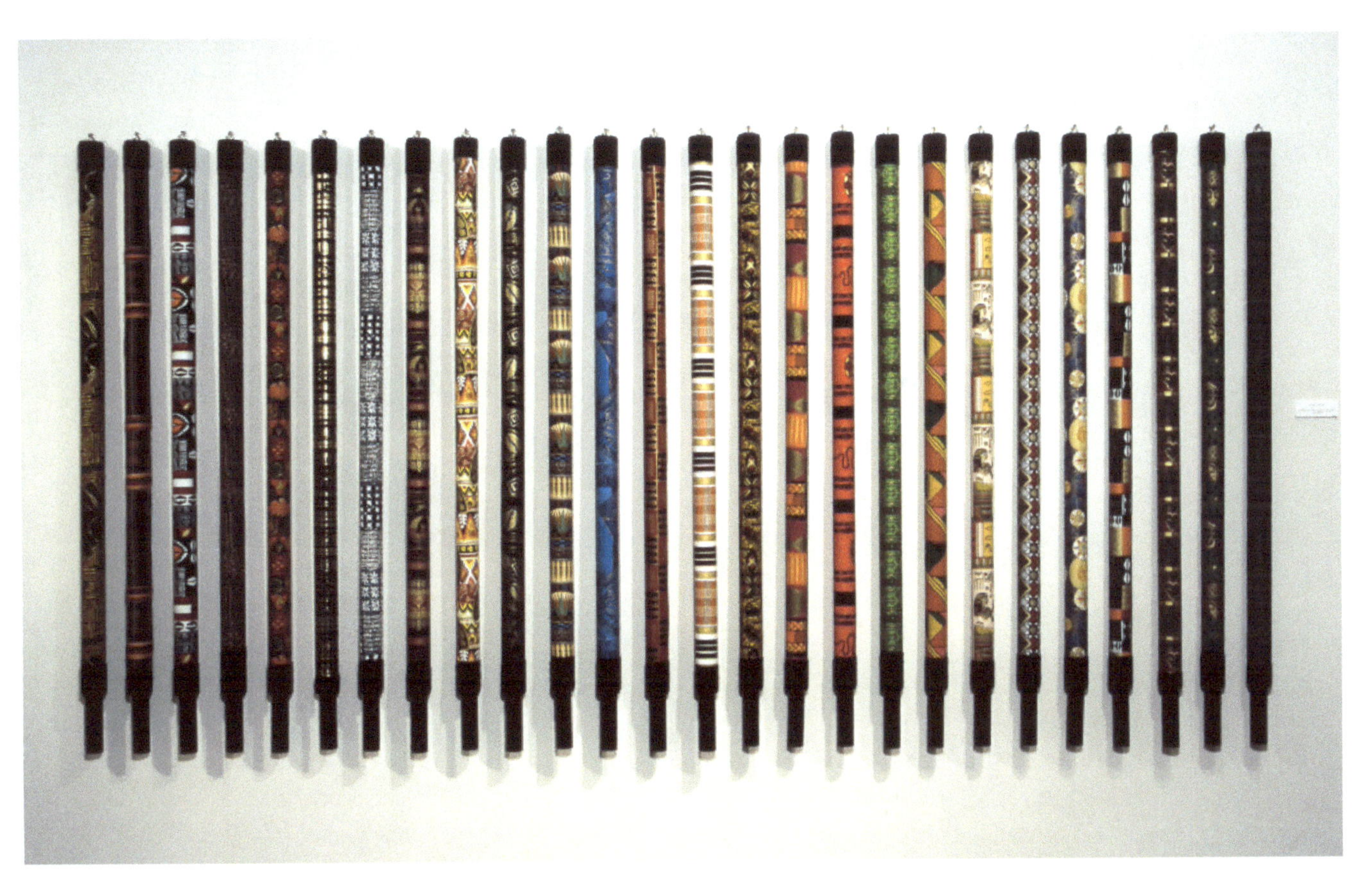

A Garland of Praise Songs for Rosa Parks , Lester Johnson

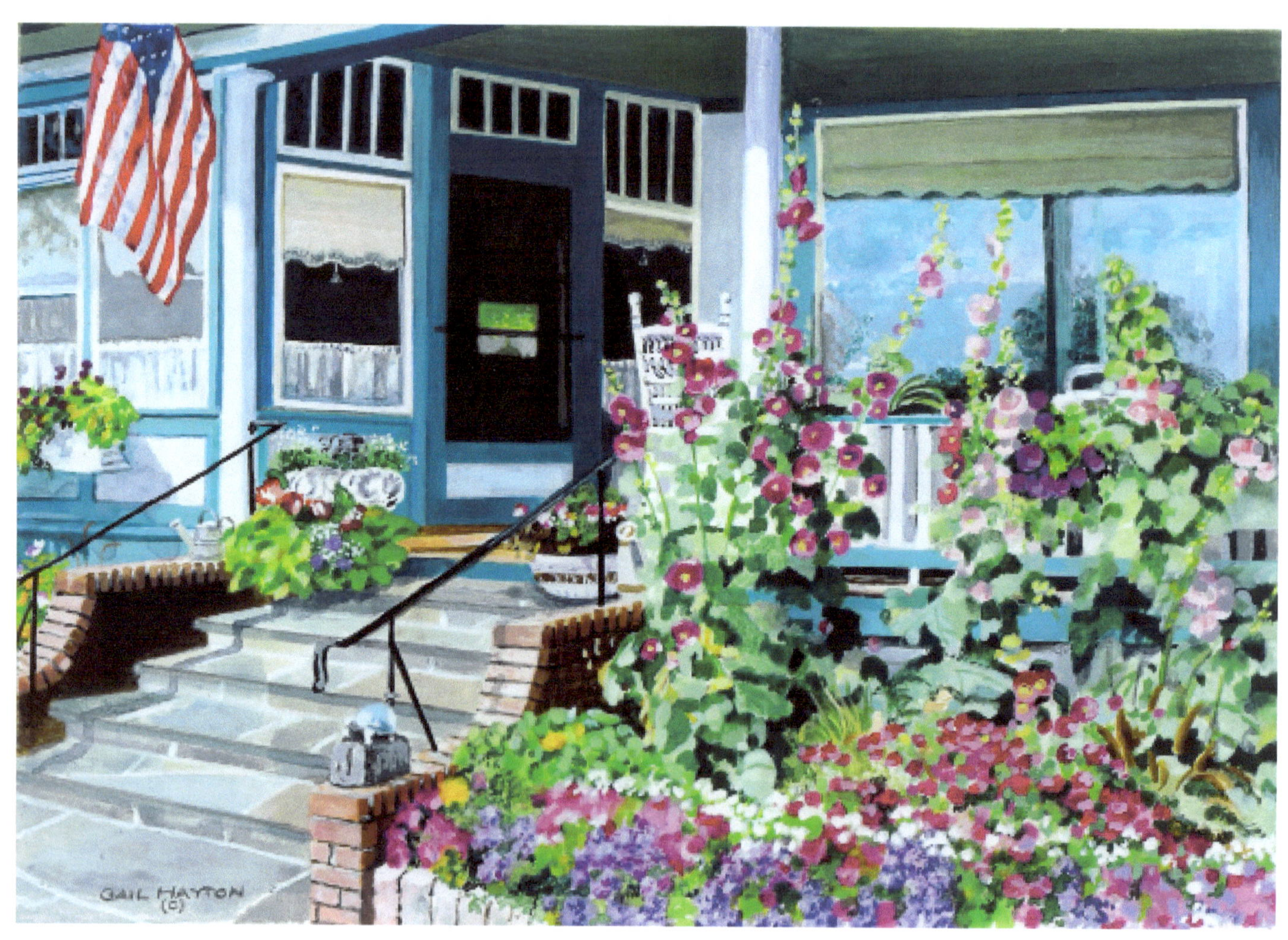

Hollyhock Heaven, Gail Hayton

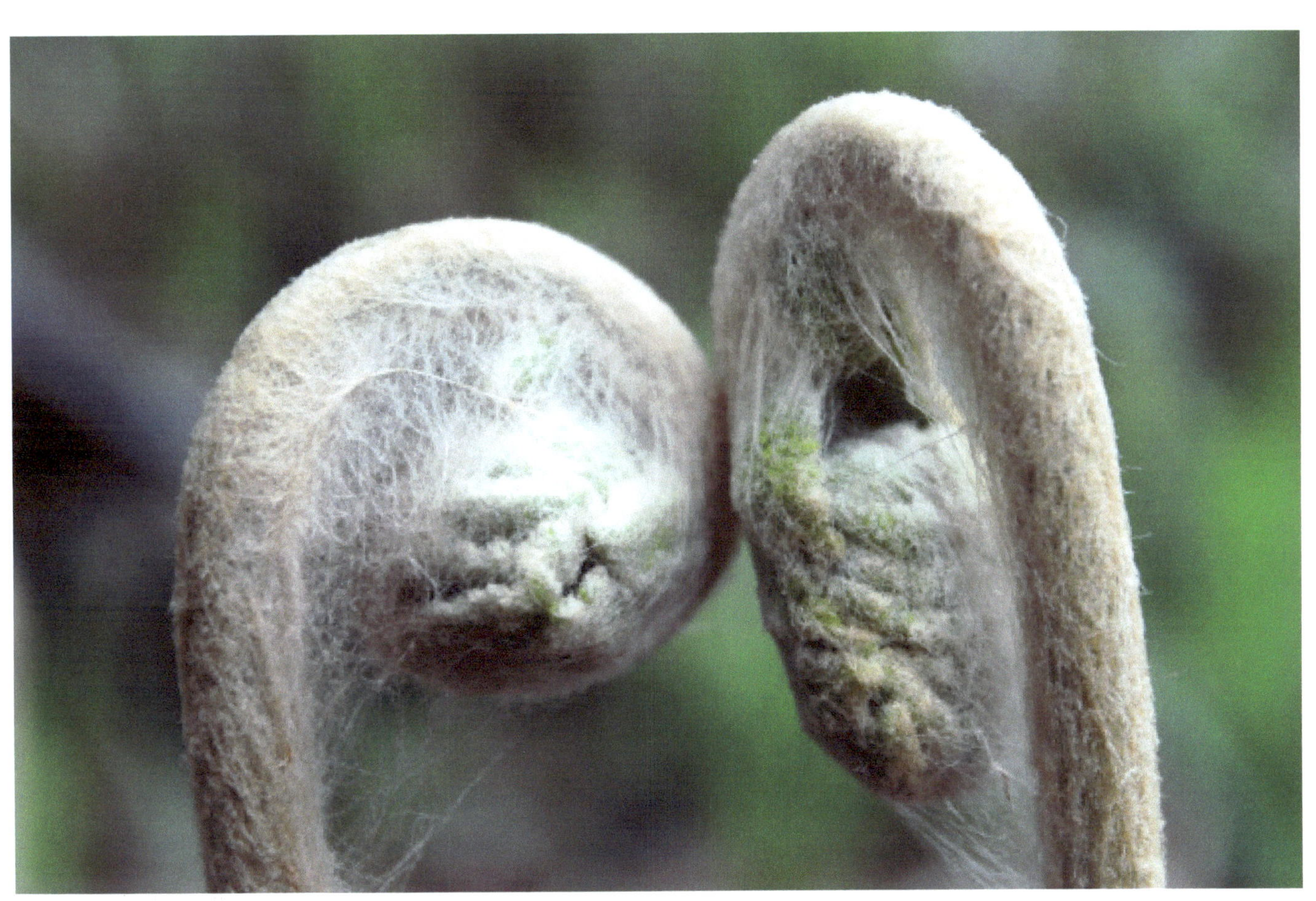

Betrothed, James Lady

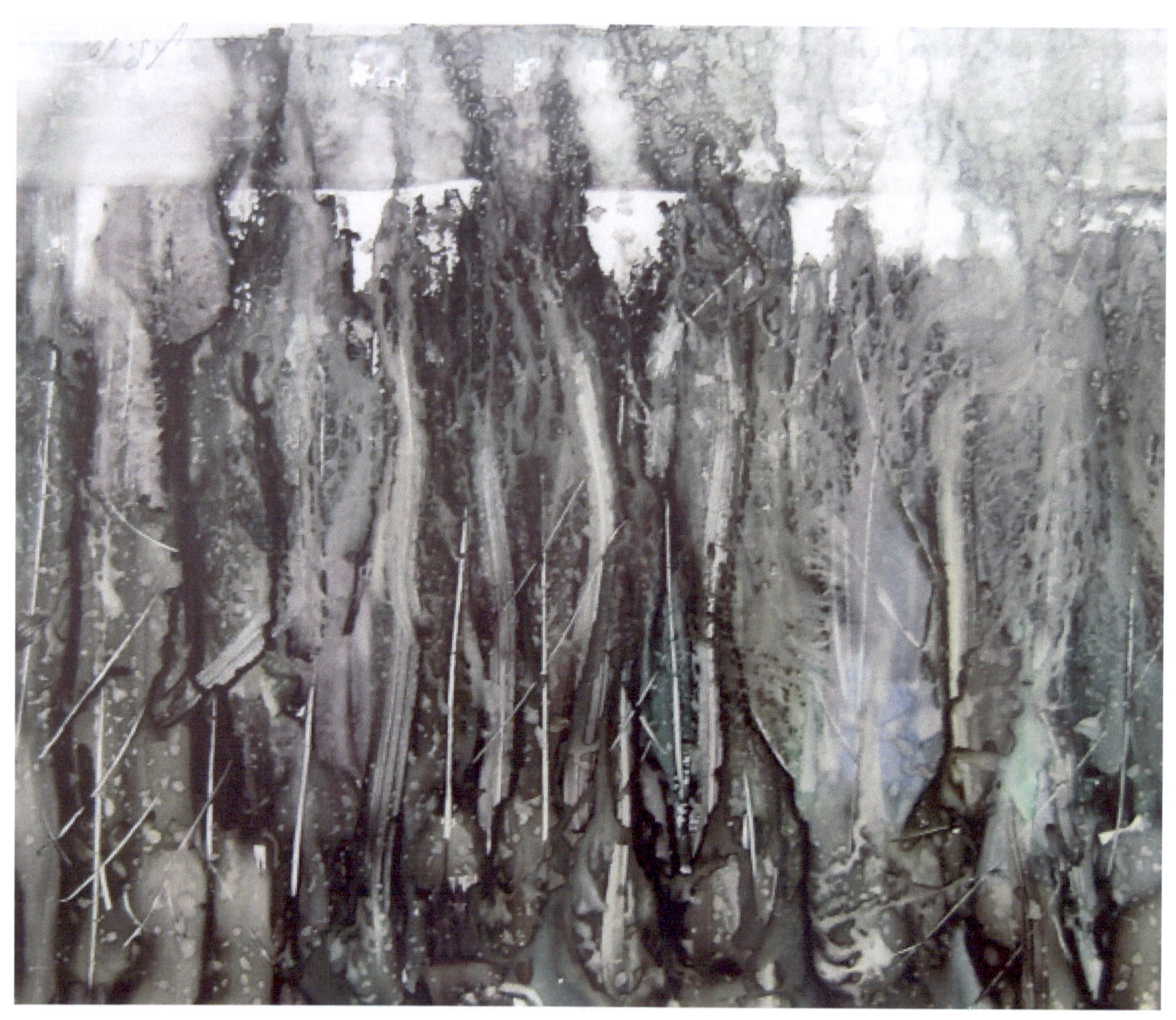

Snow in the Forest, Juergen Schmidt

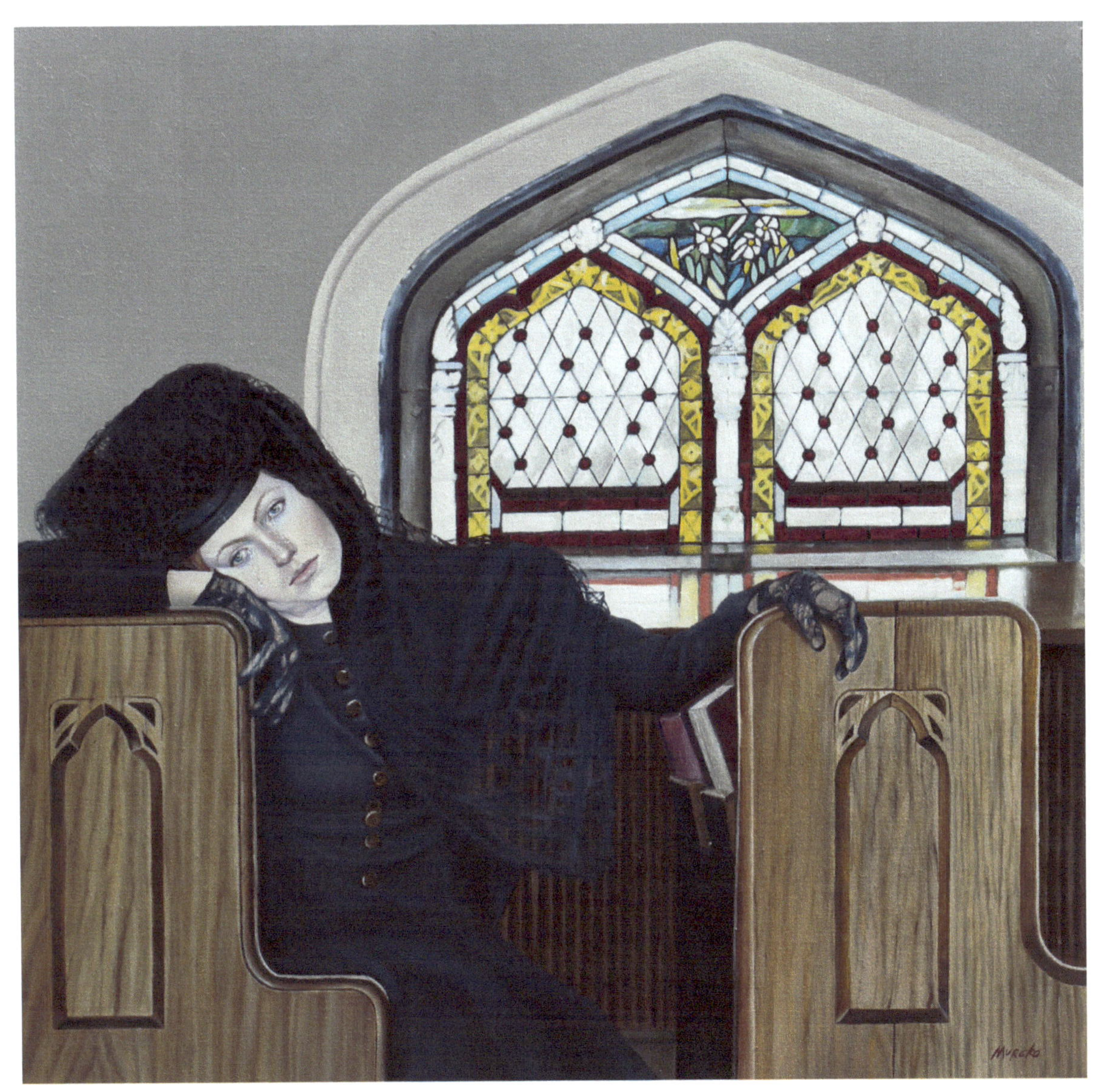

In Mourning, Bill Murcko

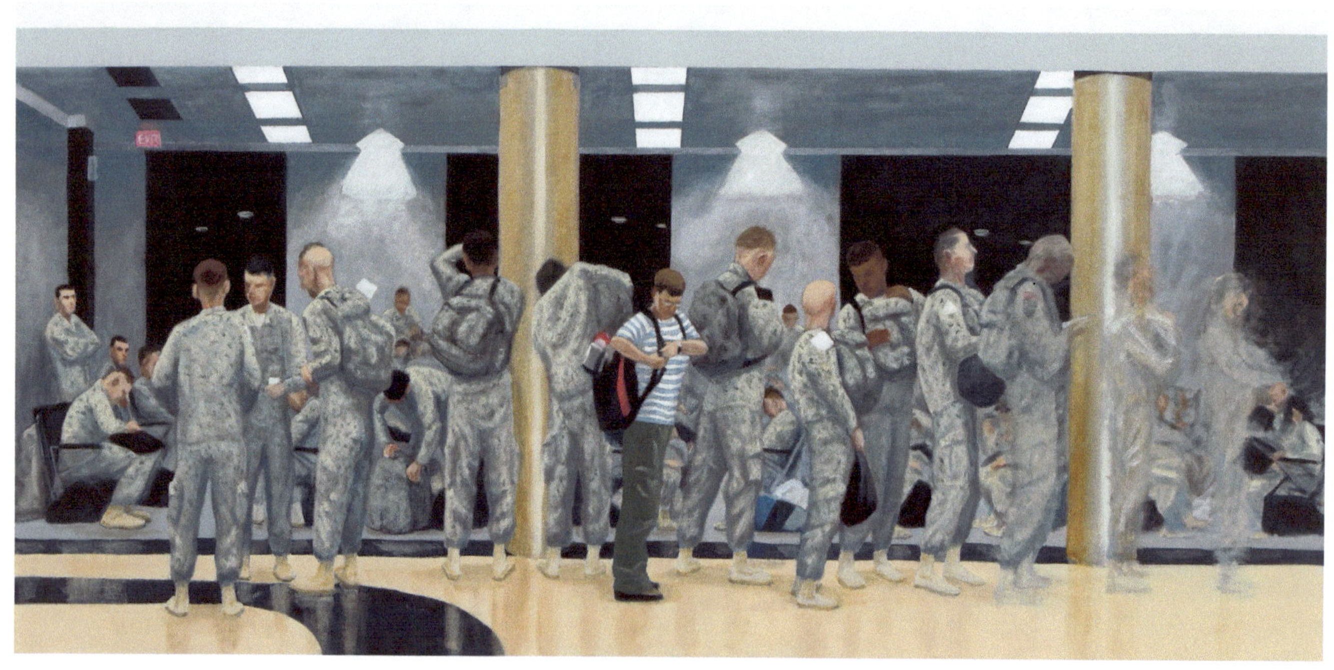

Atlanta Airport, Julie Sabit

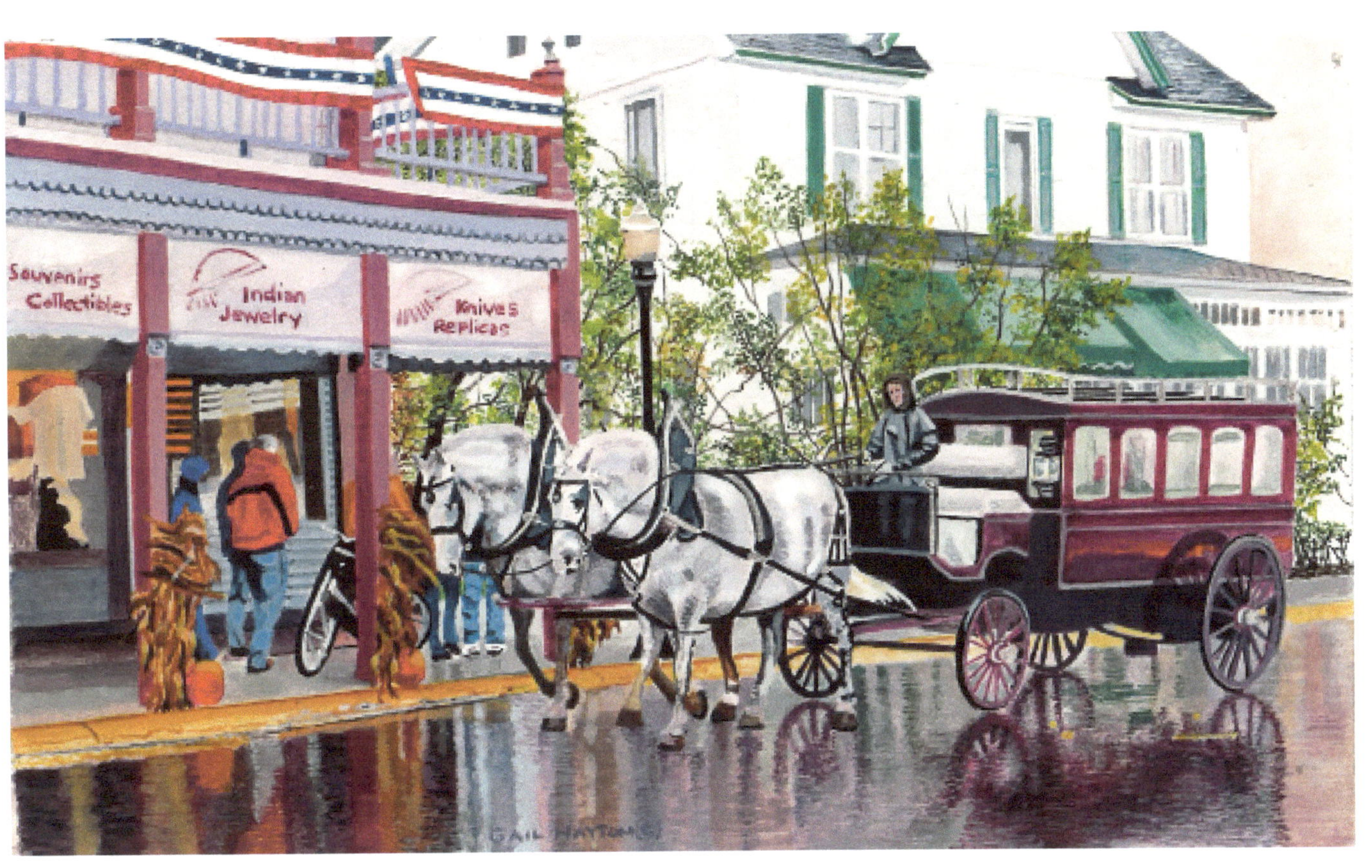

Rain on Main, Gail Hayton

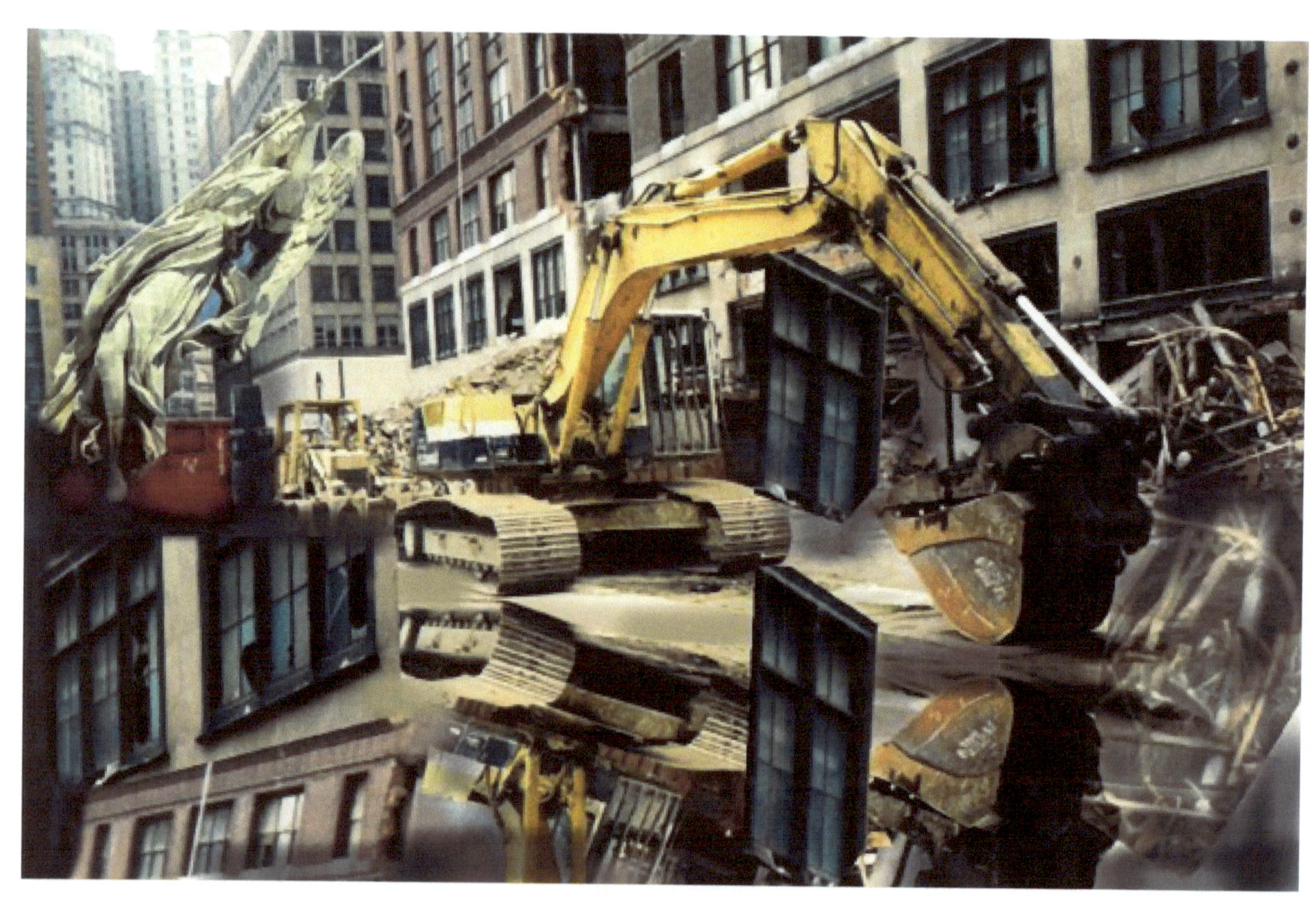

Downtown, George Booth

blueprint of a lie

VATO

gears grinding away in the head
promoting impulses relaying intentions
clouded by controversy
and covered in mud

lines connected
equating to sentences and phrases
fail to sustain meaning
in a vacuum

dials turning circuits
connecting adjectives, adverbs,
prepositional phrases
exhibiting intentions
known otherwise to the self
powered by feelings within
the body
the blood
nerves
and winds carrying messages
from exterior mechanisms

intentions for constructions
not laid on the chopping block
but perpetuated through words
spoken in encrypted form

thoughts rotate from feelings
and emotions
to actions and consequences
from the oration

thoughts rotate from feelings
and emotions
to actions and consequences
from the oration

calculated in the stages
is the pain ratio
and weighed against
the self-interest advantages claimed

the math is done
and the words are assimilated
in a phrase
carried from the neurons
and the impulses in the brain
to the vocal cords
and the lips
and expressed in the words
i
love
you

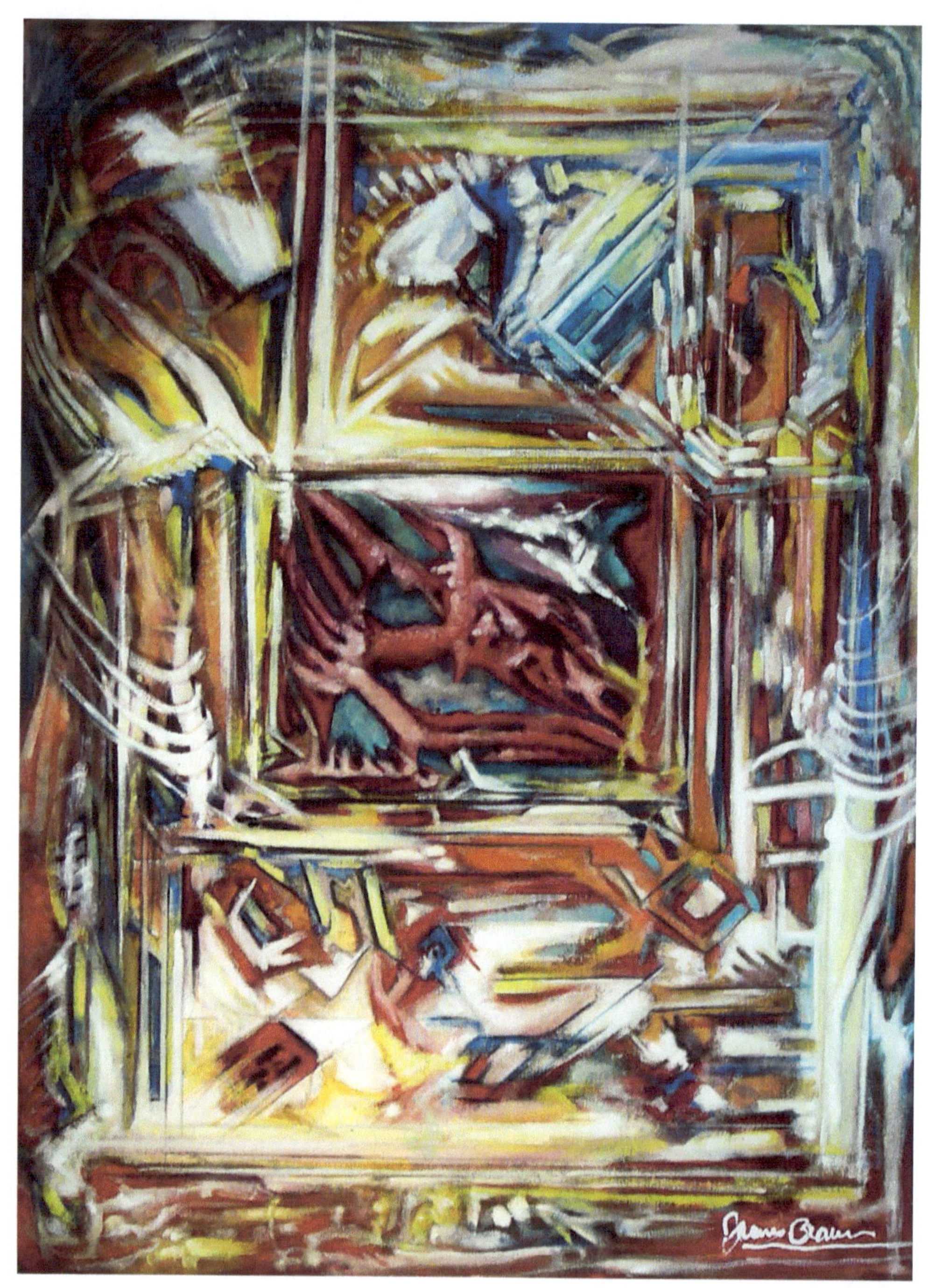

Zen Zone, James Homer Brown

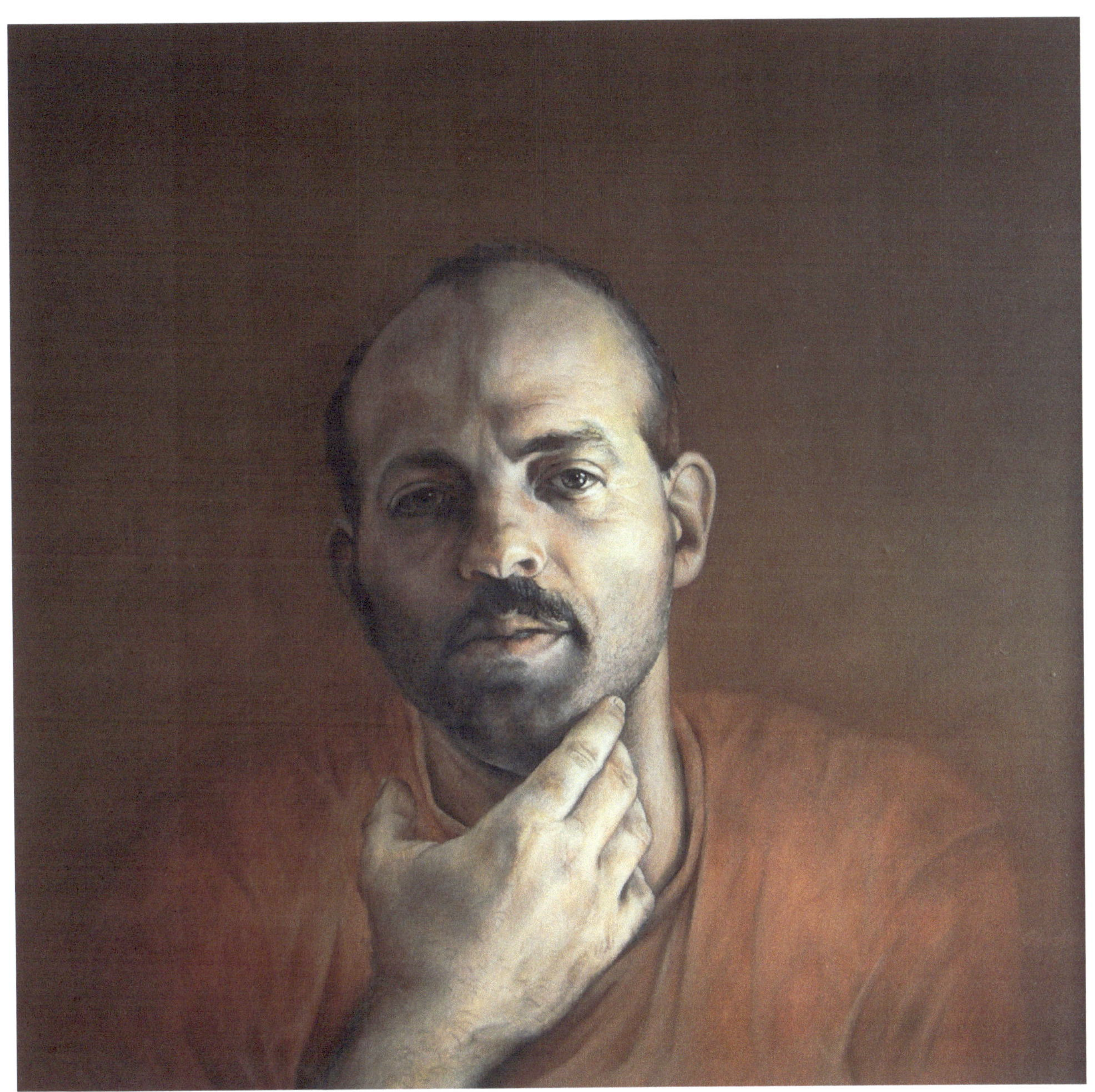

Portrait of a Friend, G. Jesse Gledhill

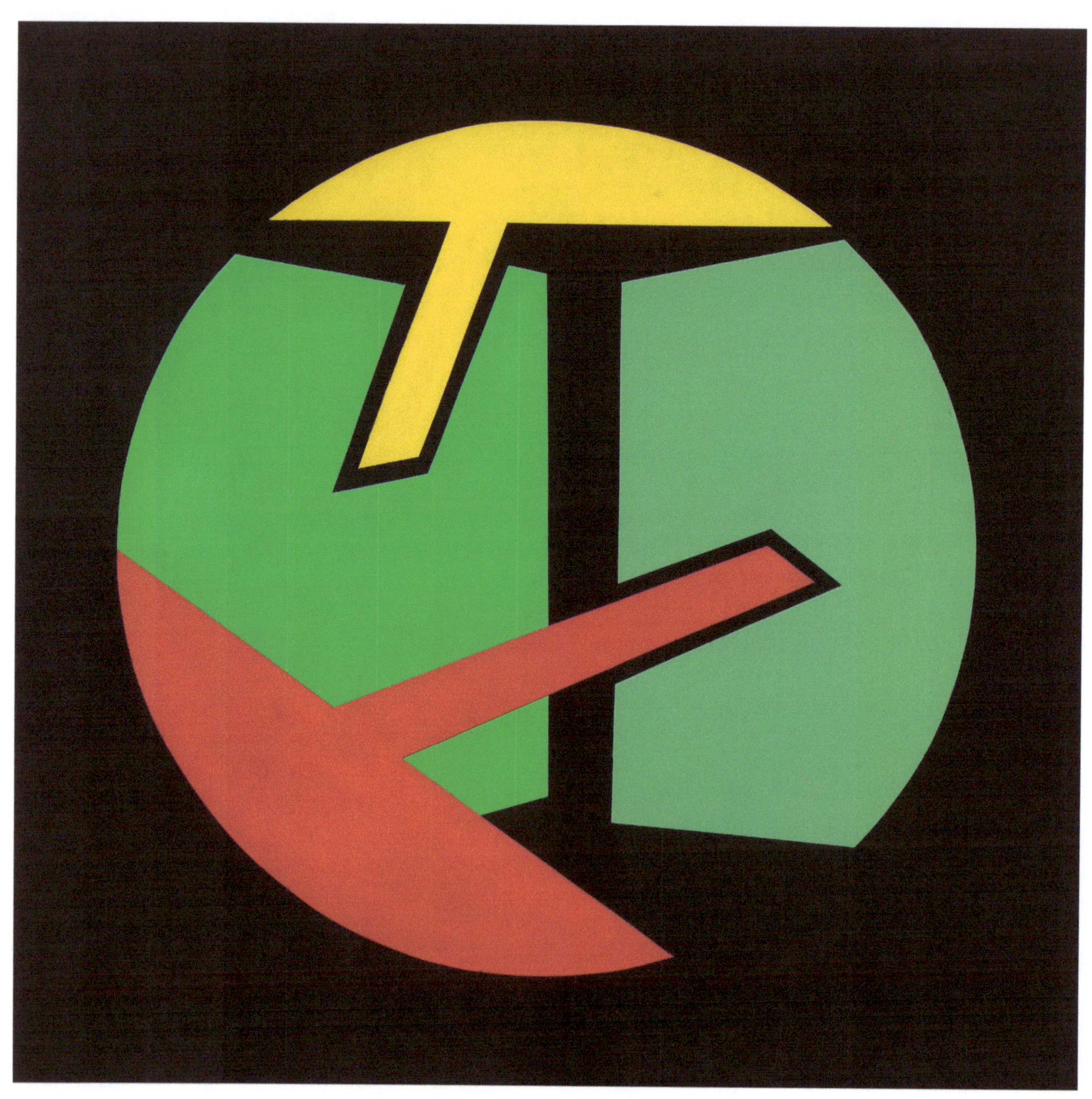

Circle Series IV, Jerald Mitchell

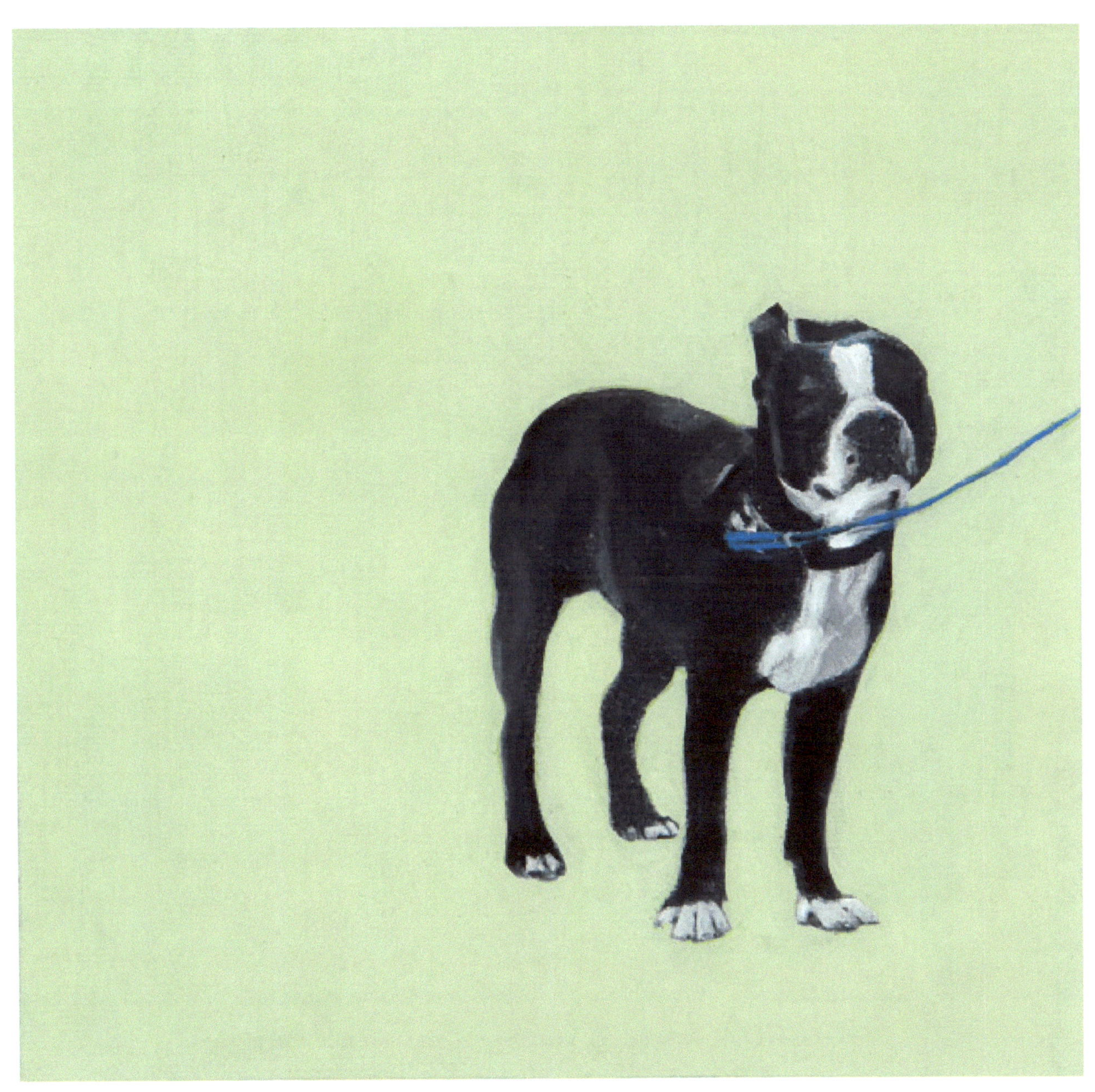

Monroe River Walk 2, Jeanne Bieri

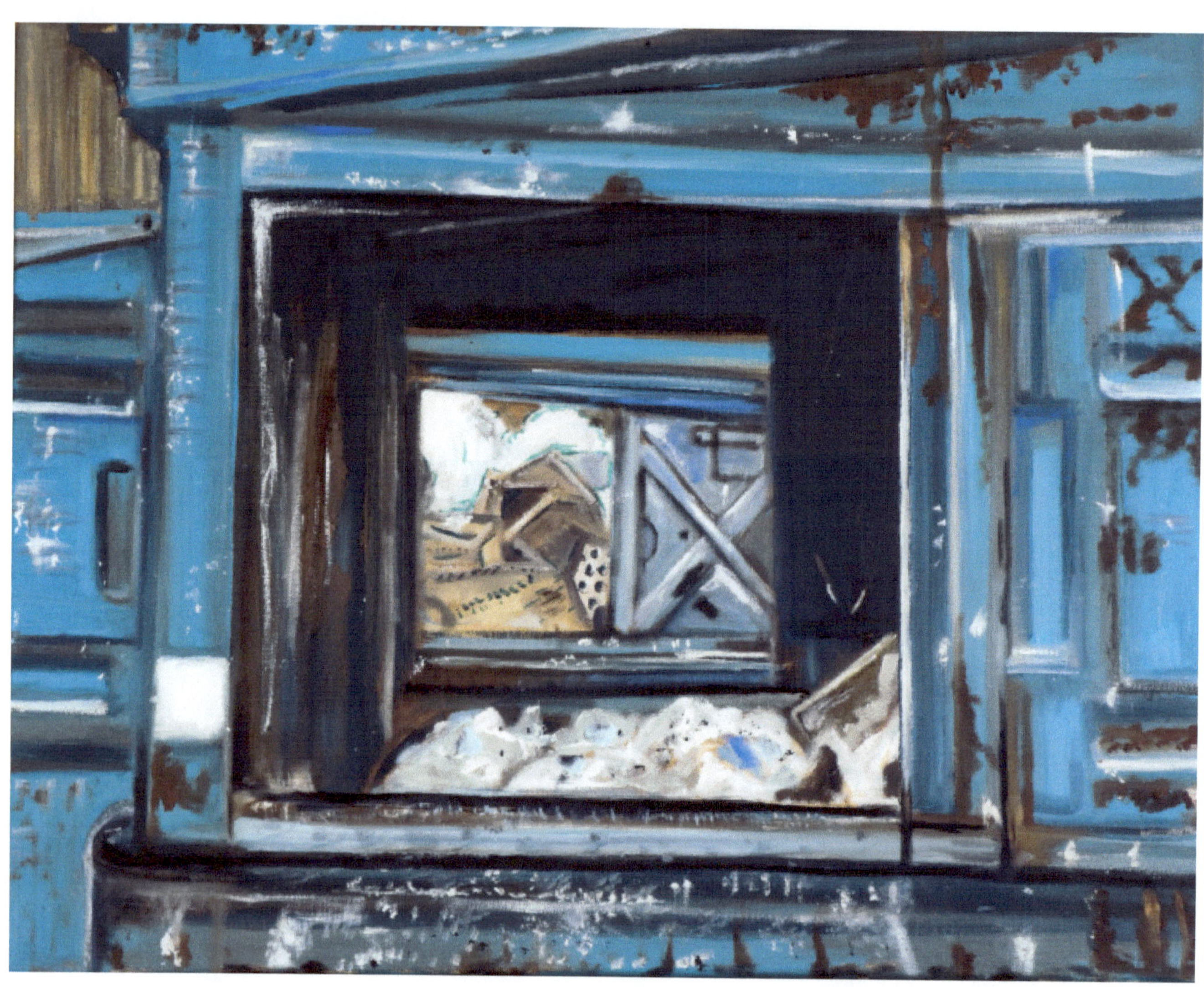

GIGO (Garbage In, Garbage Out), Agnes Gira

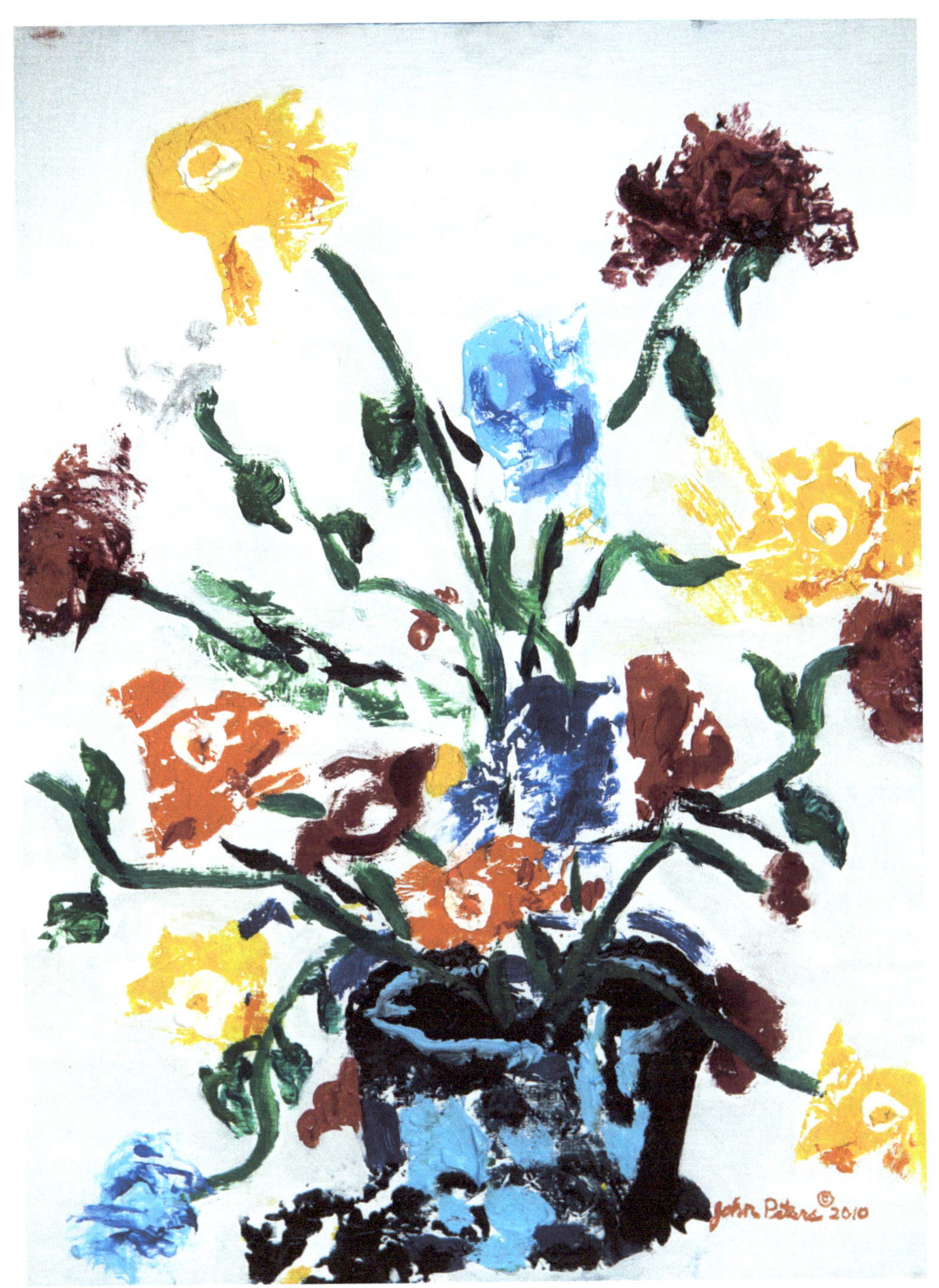

Blue Pot, John Peters

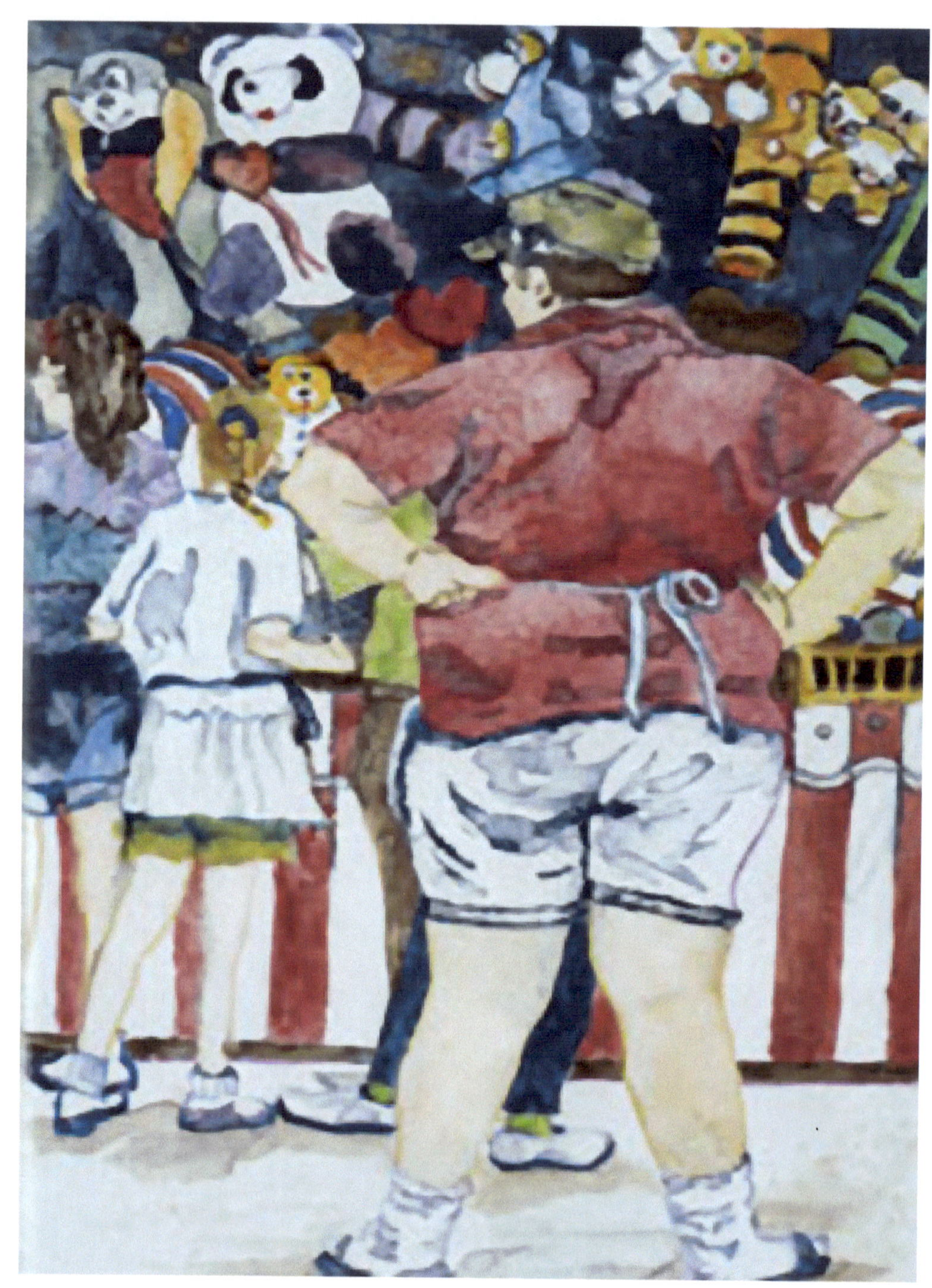

At the Fair, Jean Thomas

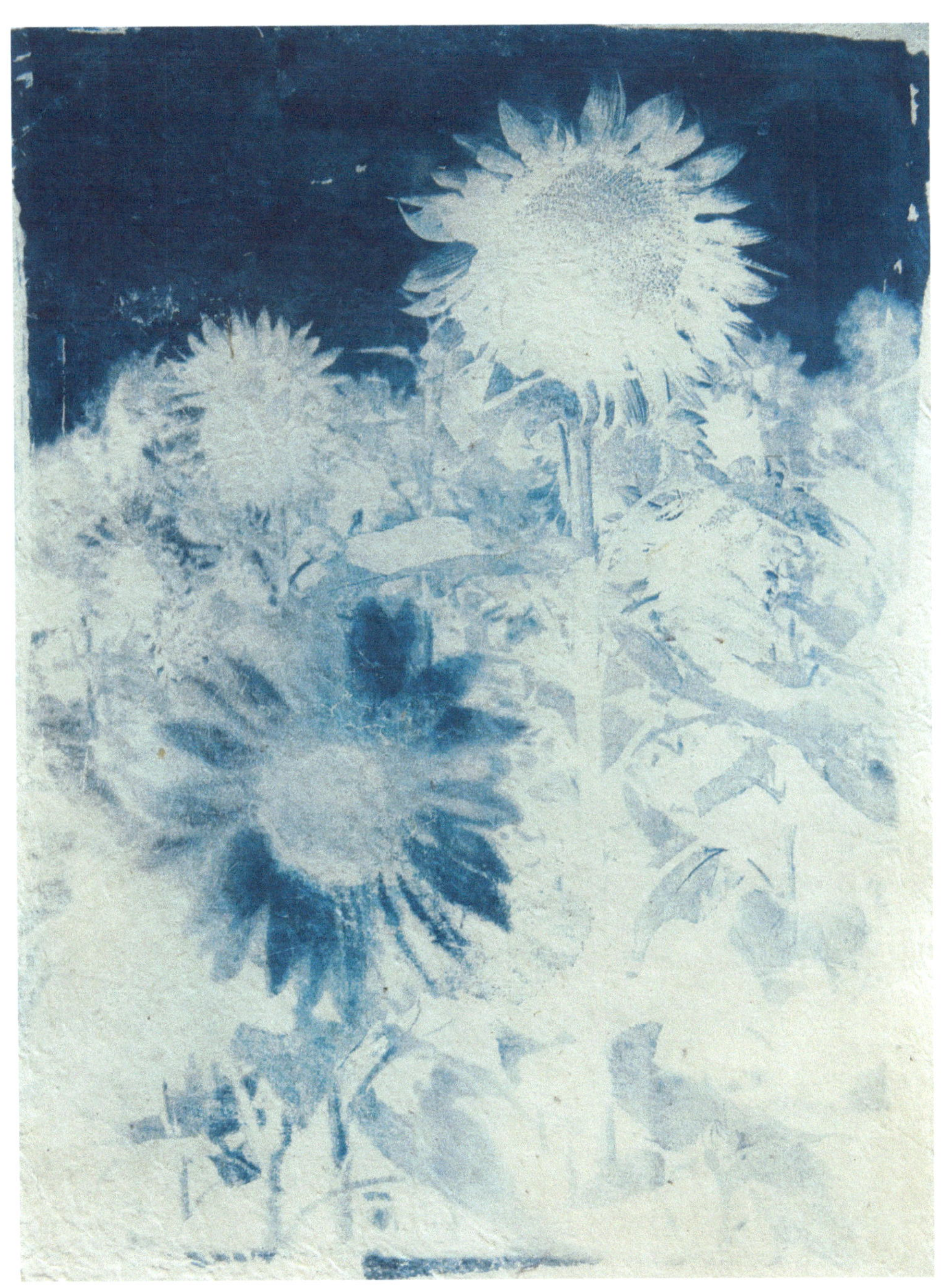

Blue Summer, Candace Law

My heart tells me something different
Karla Joy Huber

Many things we've been taught to believe
by institutions we're told don't deceive.
But my heart tells me something different.

We're taught that if it's not one it's always the other
That if God's not a woman He's a man
That Creator couldn't possibly be both or neither
But my heart tells me something different.

We're told "politically correct" is about making amends
But at the same time, enemies can never become friends
But my heart tells me something different.

We're told there's only one way
one correct definition
one correct history,
regarding the Creator
But my heart tells me something different.

They say you can't have both
It can't be both
It just wouldn't work to try and take turns
That every person under present system gets what she or he earns
But my heart tells me something different.

We're told that because it's "always" been done that way,
it's worthy of respect for that alone
But my heart tells me something different.

They say ailments can be isolated and treated as self-contained
That there's a medical treatment for every kind of pain
That "enhancements" are life-improving rather than just vain
They say physical science is all that's required for a healer to be adequately trained
But my heart tells me something different.

They say if you can't see it it's not true
that old is never as good as new
and that much is always better than few
that one can't be trained to see through another view
— But that can't be true, because I just met you, and I'm guessing that your heart told you something different.

I heard it said that love can be described but never defined
That to one word it can't be confined
that it comes in many more forms than are usually comprehended
or considered by the Western mind.
This my heart told me to be true.

It doesn't make sense to value life and war
at the same time
To believe in peace and play games based on crime
No more than it does to expect a tank to stop on a dime.
It doesn't make sense for Creator to put so much work into making this world
just to be a miserable stopping point
and for death from it to be what's most sublime
or to believe that where we're at right now is the highest we can climb
This my heart told me to be true.

When my heart told me something different,
I didn't understand
why what I was being taught seemed so bent
and broken
and distorted

why though there were suspicions the truth was never reported
at least not to me
or to you
or to the teachers
or the preachers
or the pitiful creatures
that needed it most
to the guests
or to the hosts
and no one listened to the ghosts
who've been banished from the coasts
of our minds
lest hearing them inspire us to go find
the truth
that might help the youth
believe in something different
 than fighting, than hate
 than by violence a difference they'll make
 than when you crush an enemy, victory is what remains
 than that construction comes from self-serving destruction
 and peace from war
Because if we keep telling them that, as a species we won't get very far
Before our legacy and this earth
burn out like a dead star

So if the leaders don't change their message
to reflect what happens in real life
which is that might does not ever make right
I pray that the hearts of children,
like mine did,
will tell them something different.

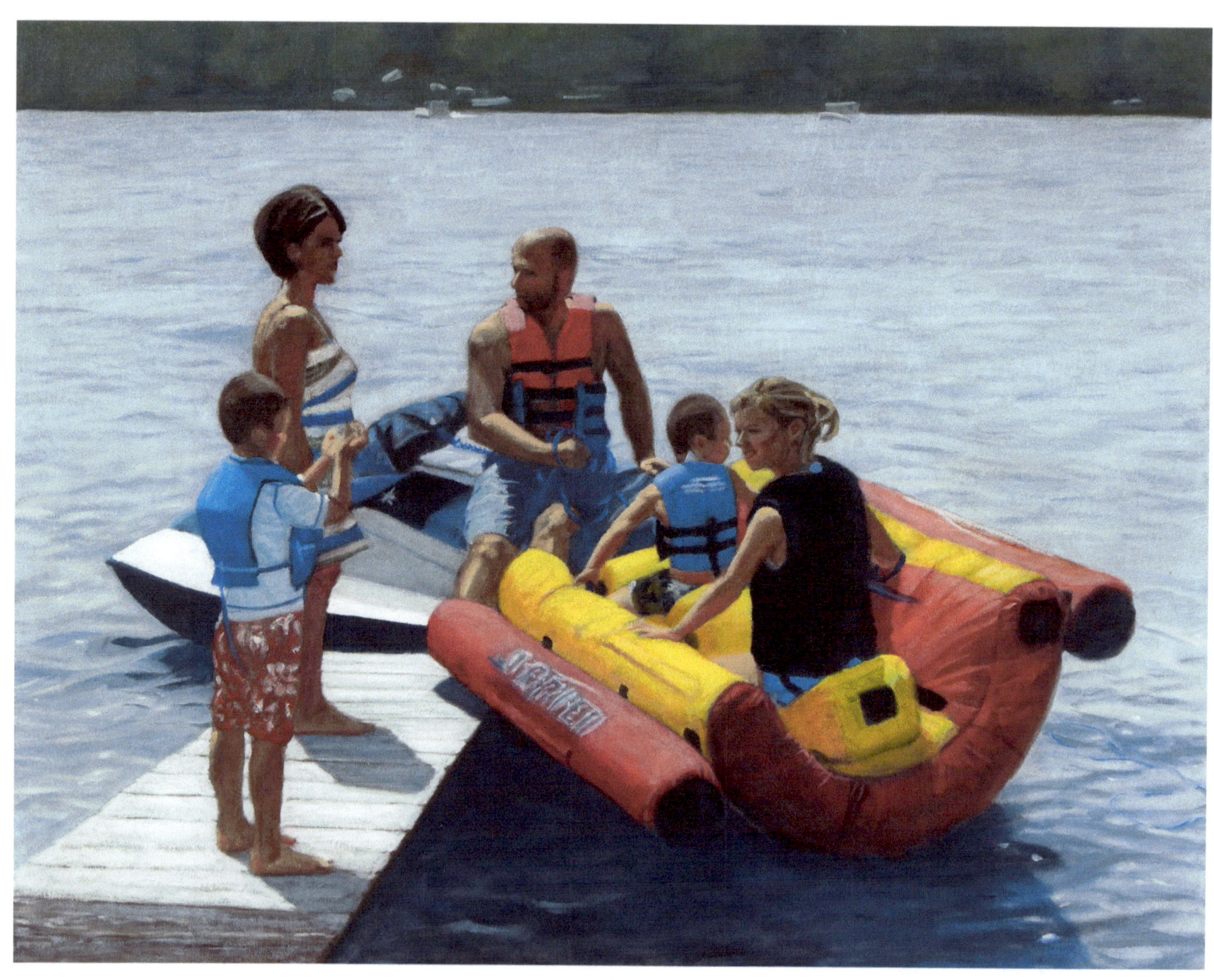

Let's Go, Julie Sabit

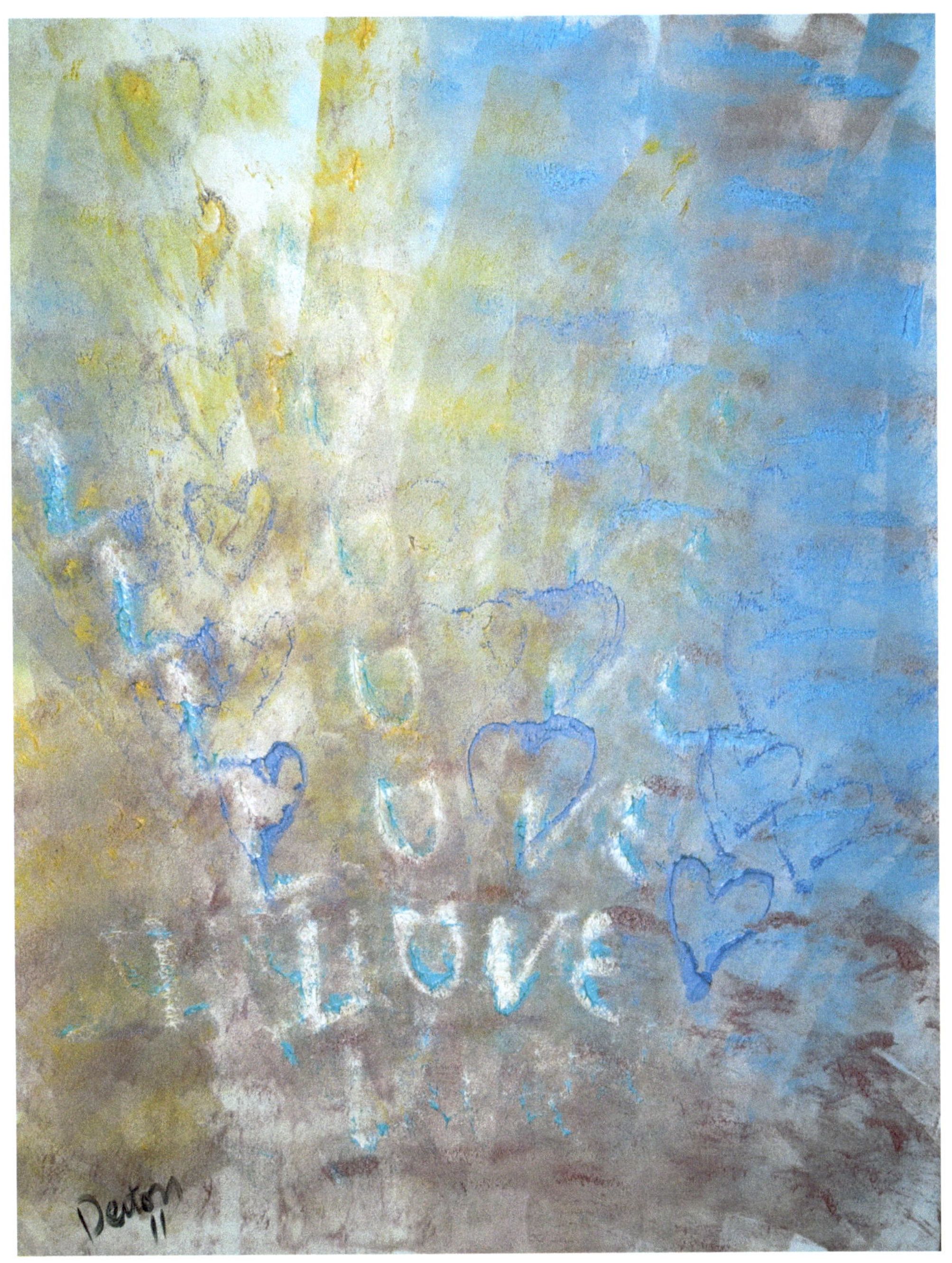

Love, Karl Denton

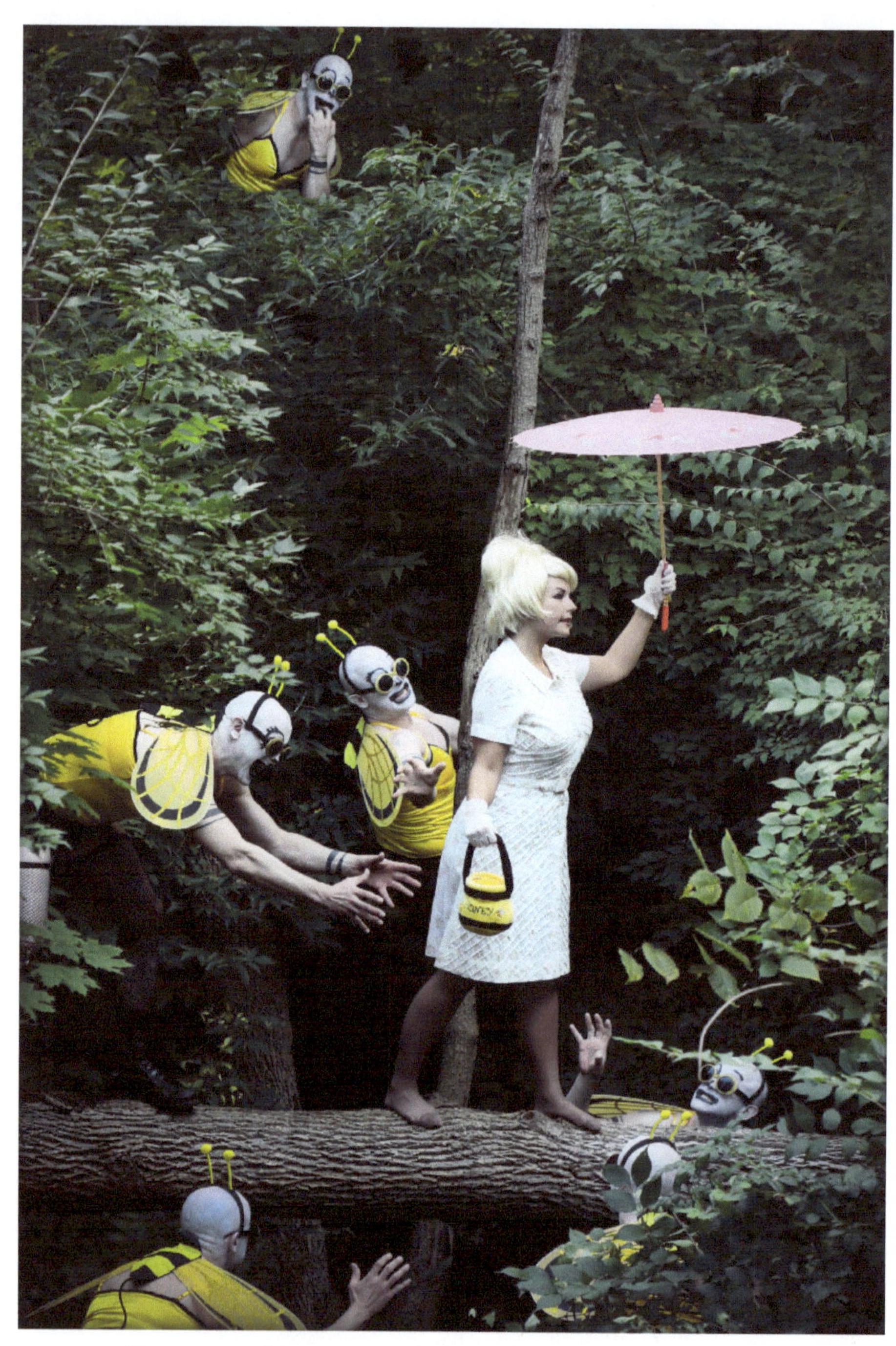

Ravenous Honeypot Stang Bang, A. Owen Layne

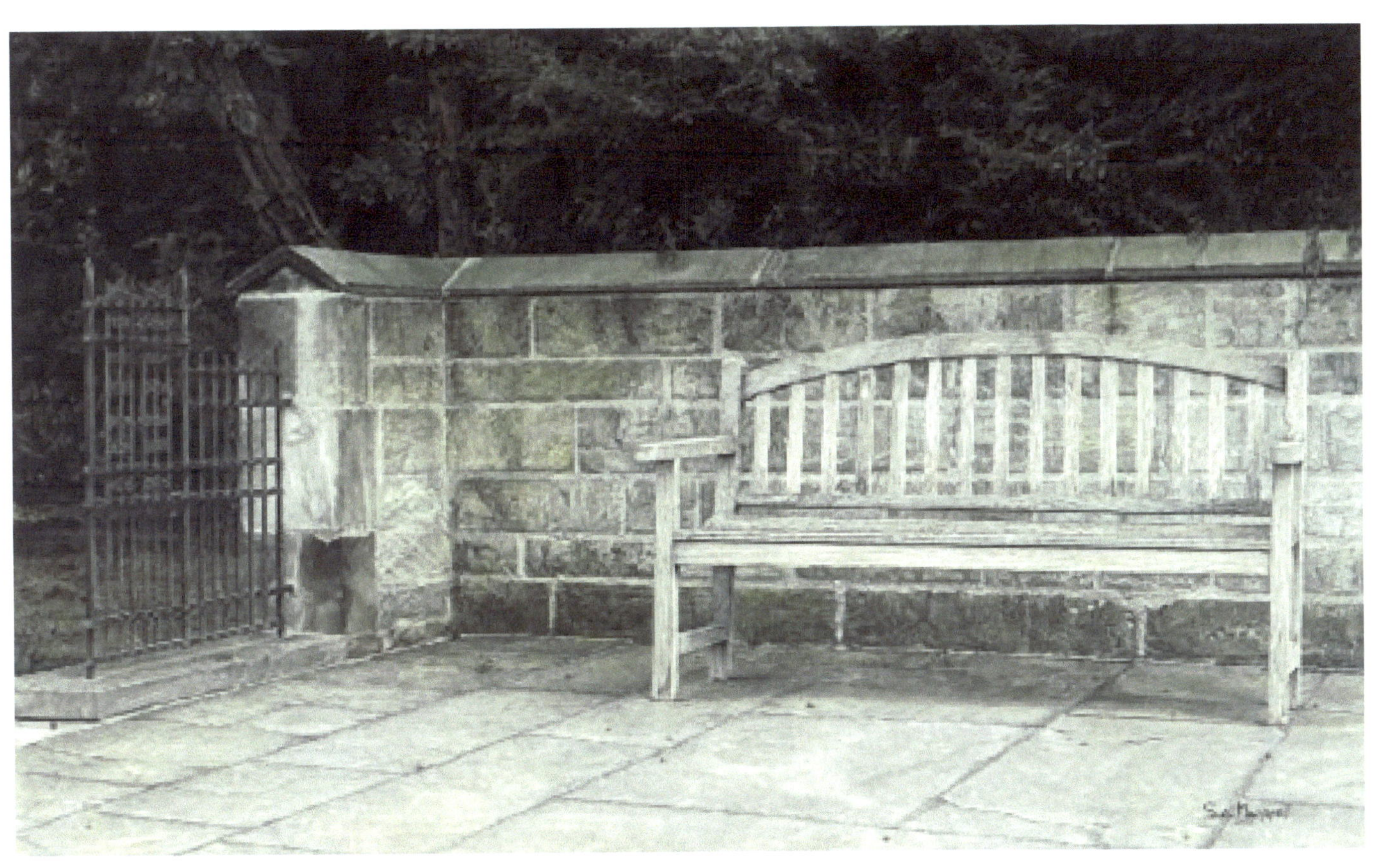

Missing Eleanor, Scott Maggart

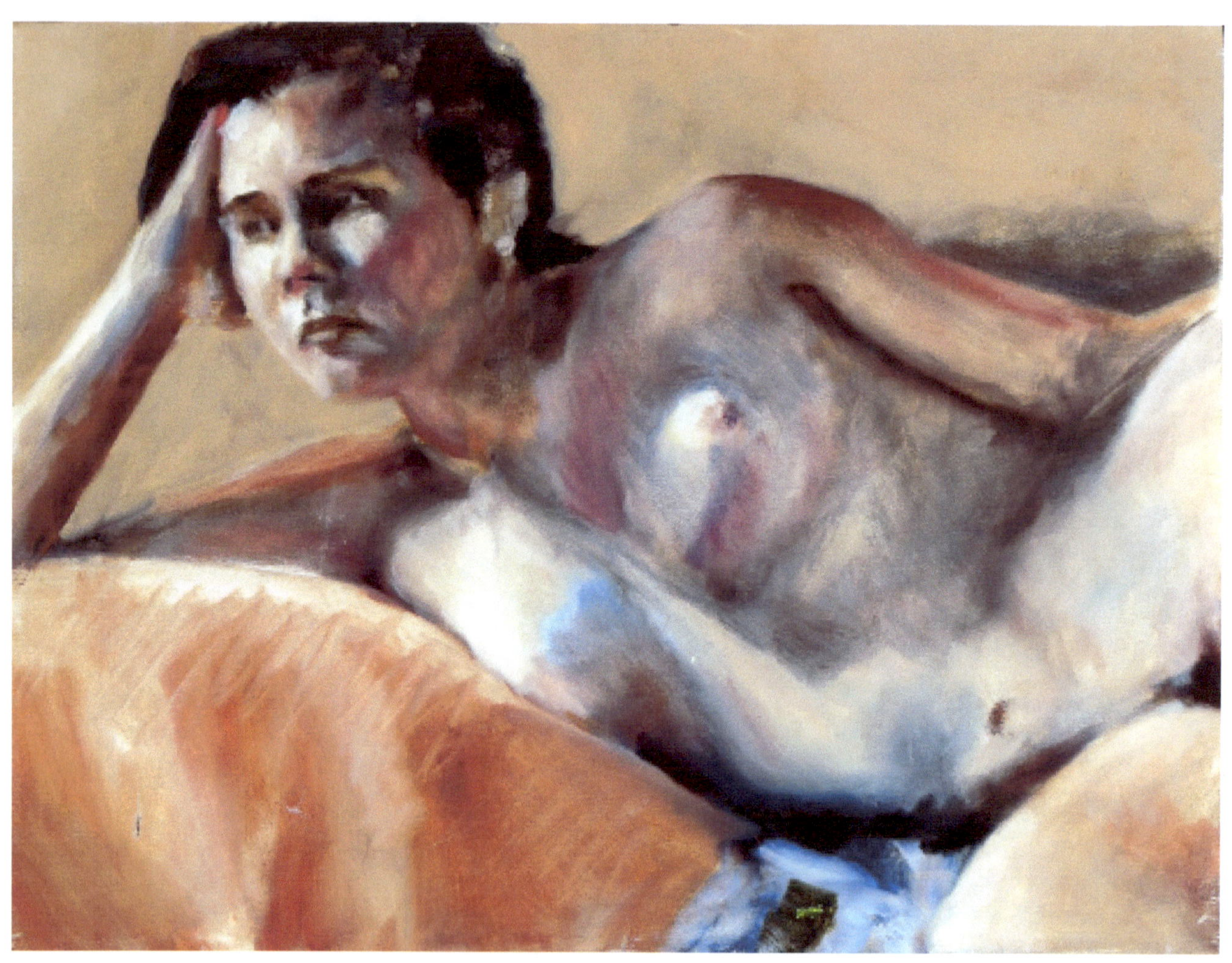

Roberta, Mike McMath

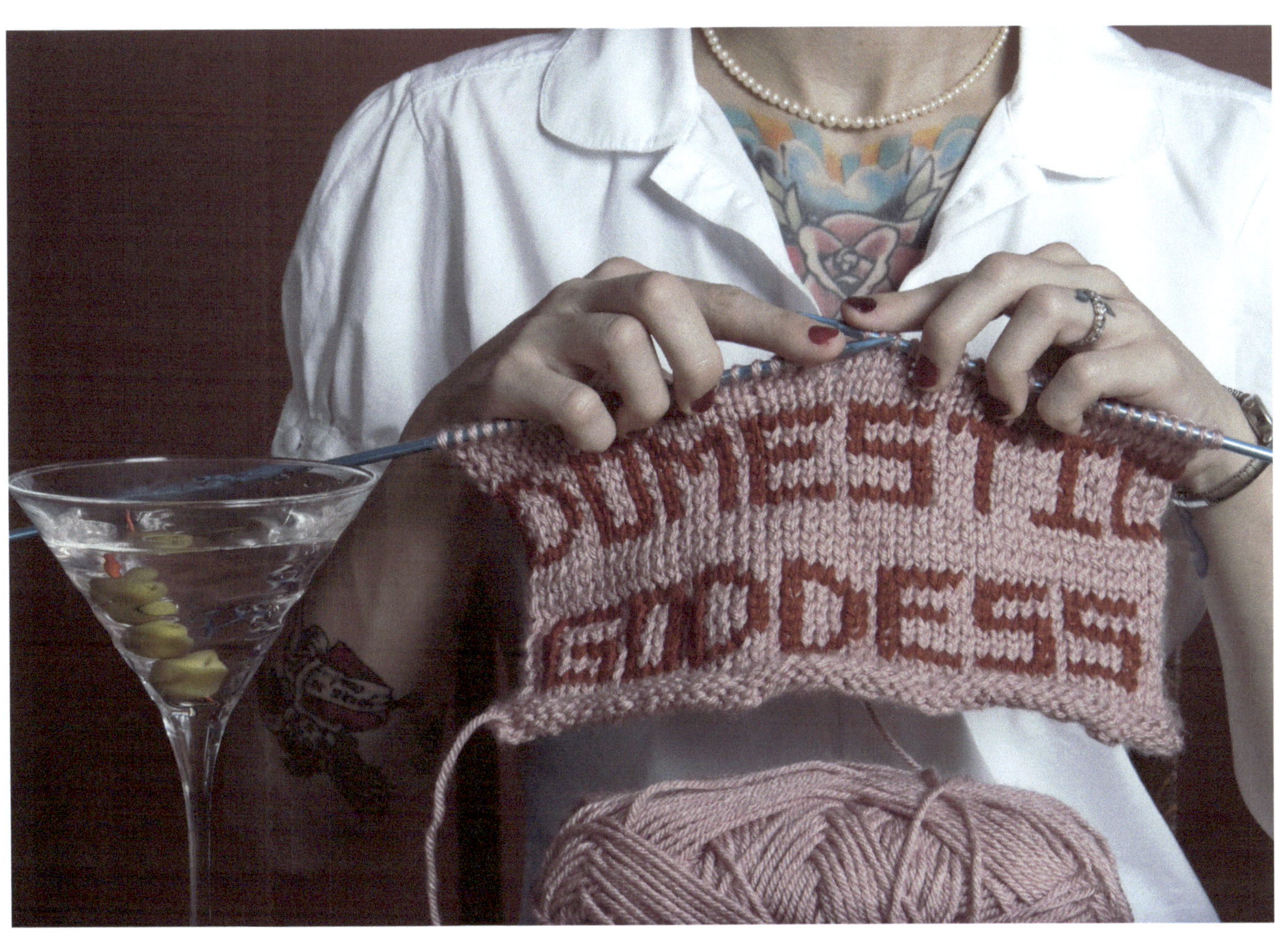

Domestic Goddess, Momcat Kelly

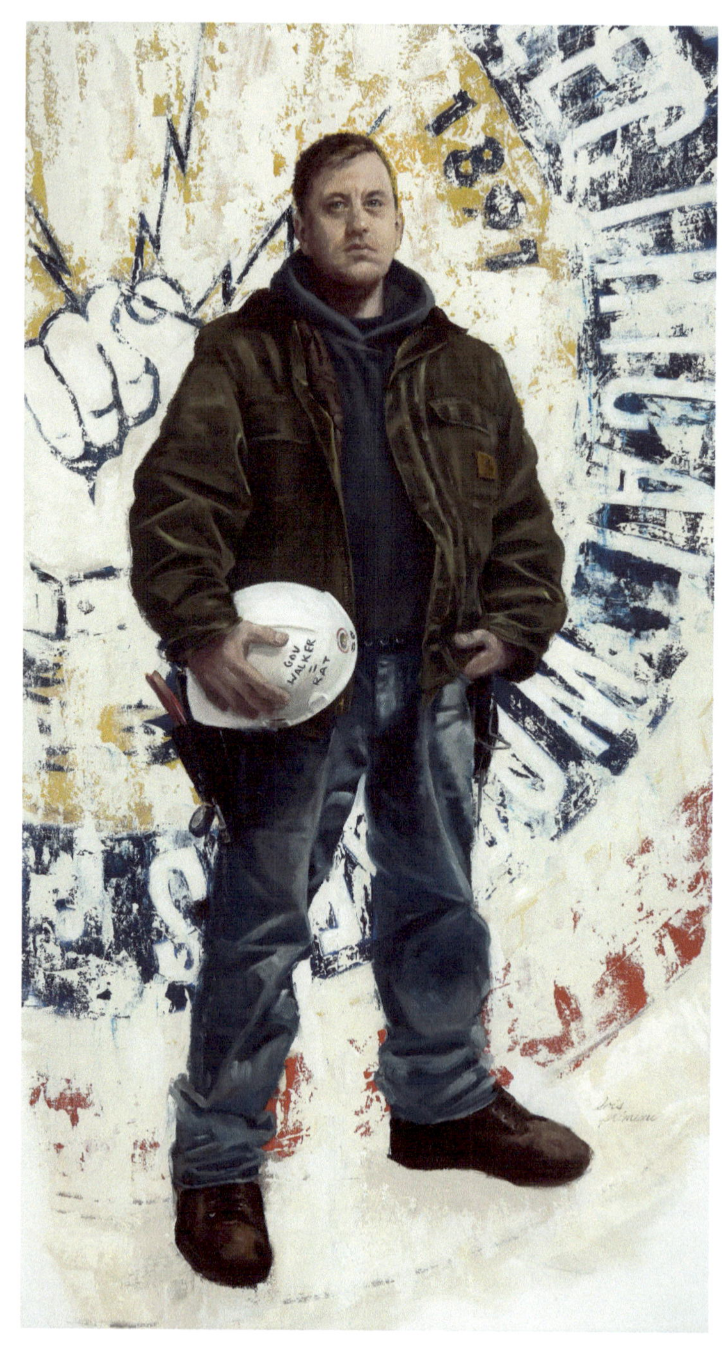

Nick, Lois Primeau

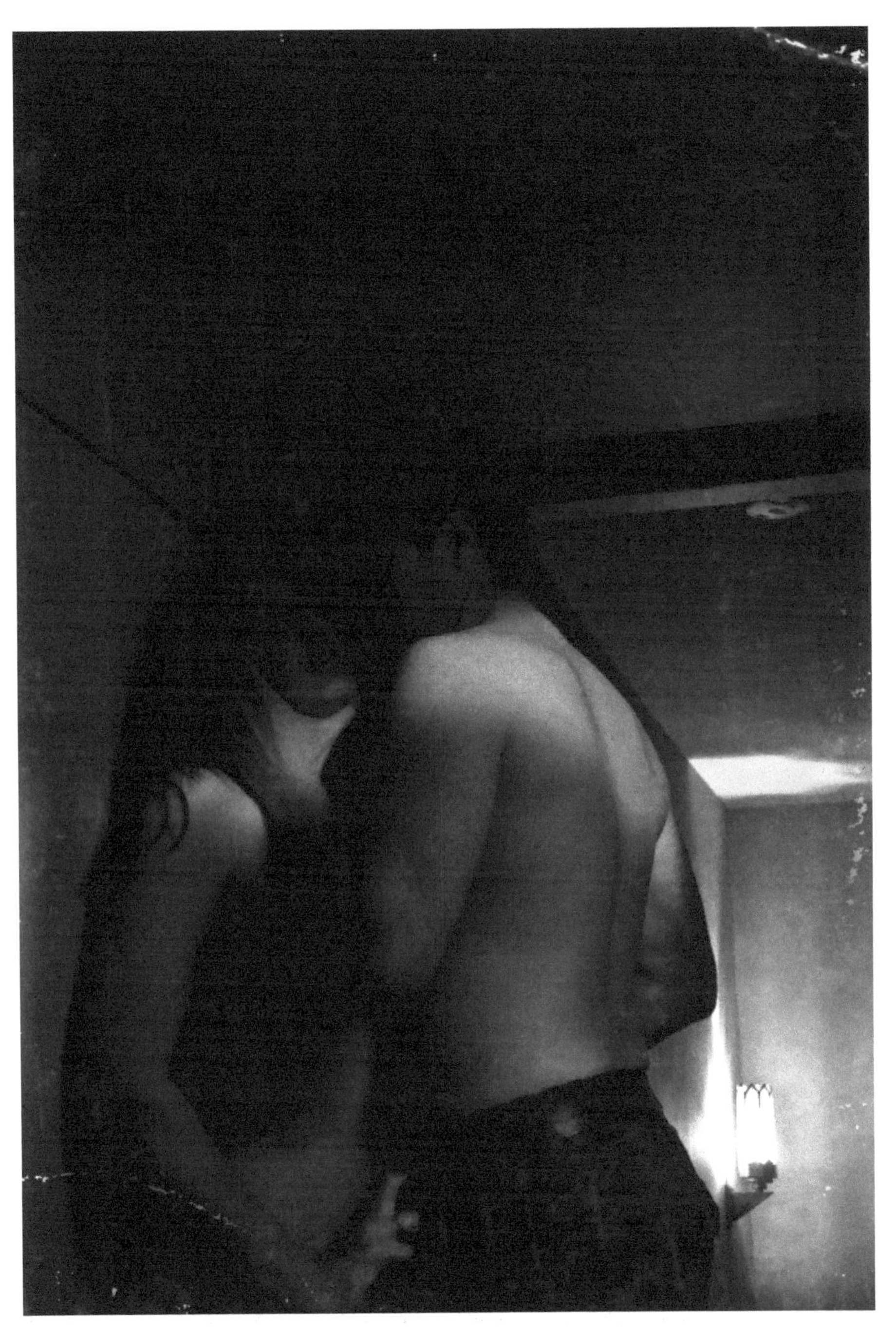

I Found A Reason, VATO

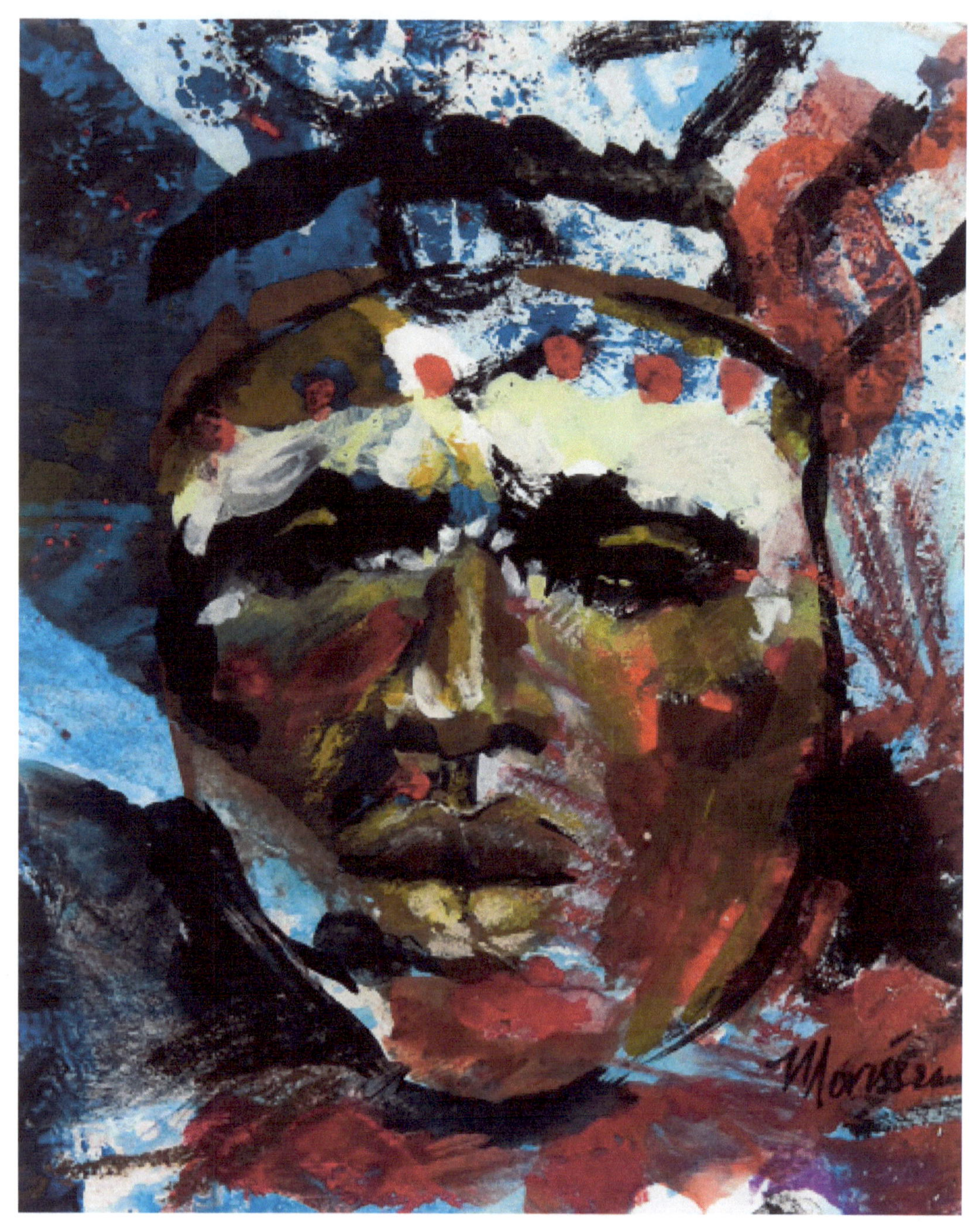

Initiation Ritual, Carole Morisseau

In Too Many Memories
Lou Cantoni

In too many memories
I walk alone down strange streets,
kick trash from city sidewalks,
ride streetcars to nowhere.
When you came, paths cleared,
forests beckoned, meadows shone.
Looks, embraces nurtured us,
we gloried in laughter.
Now you no longer care.
You avoid me, wear somber clothes

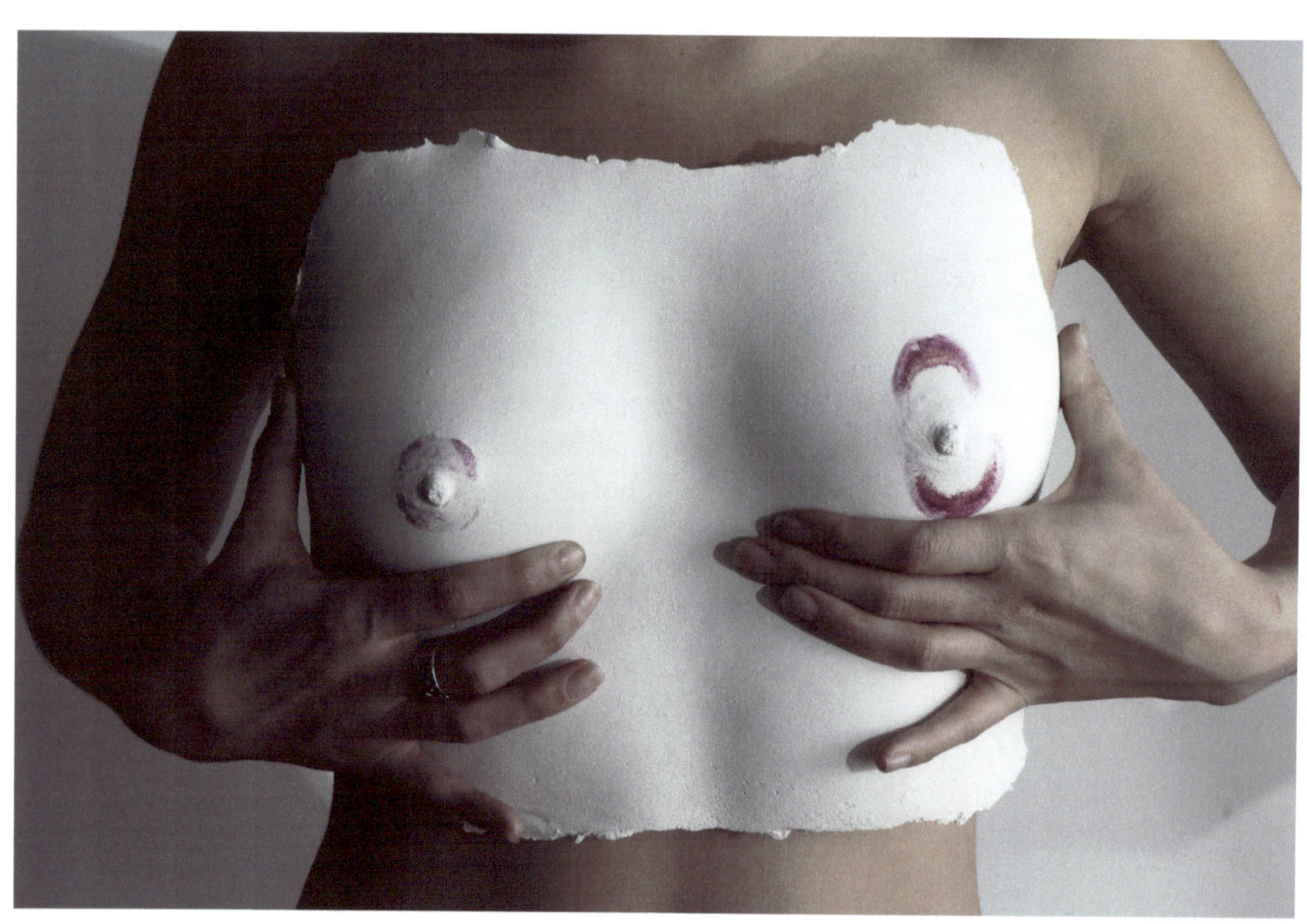

Self Love, Karl Denton

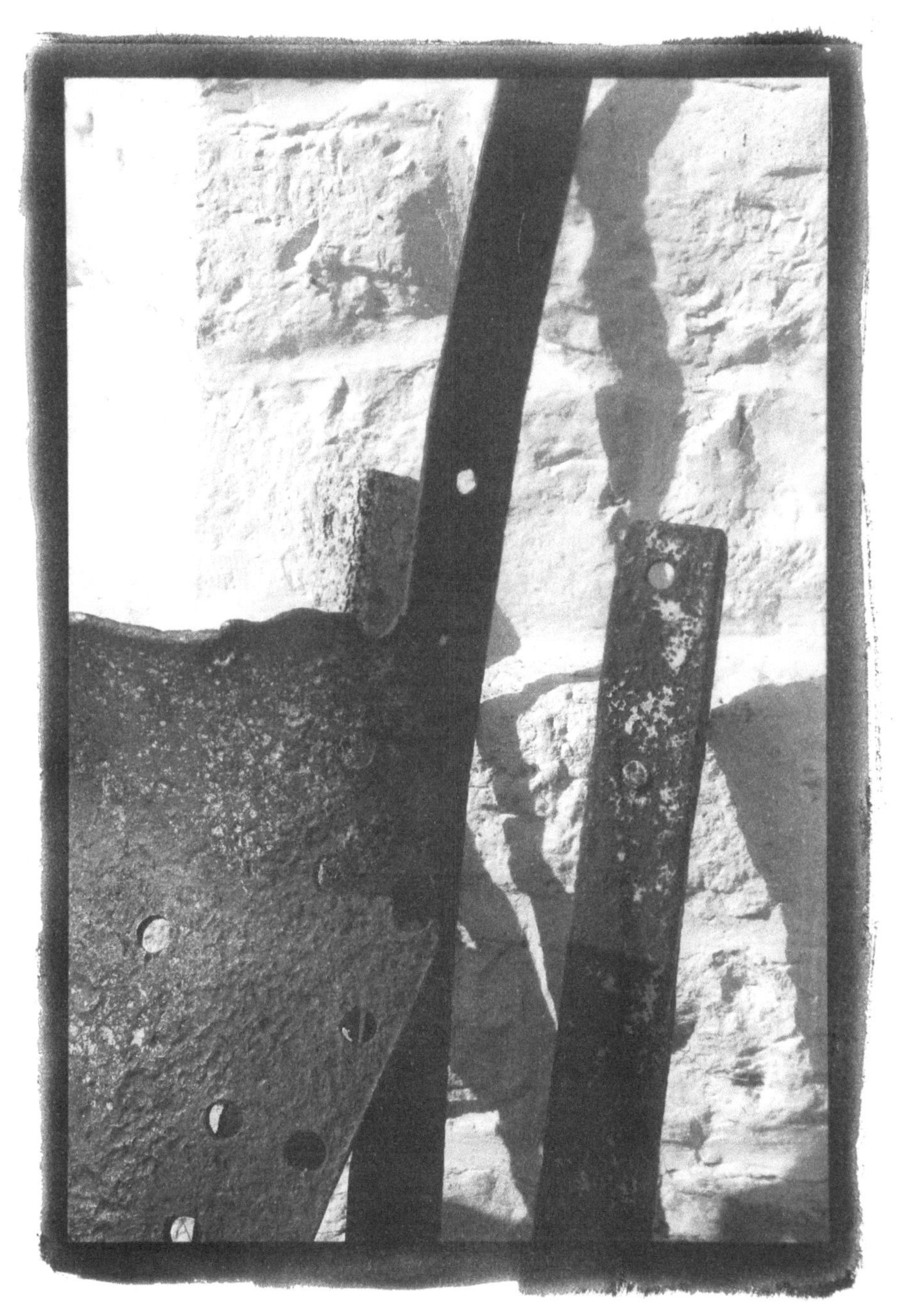

Broken Plow, Eric Law

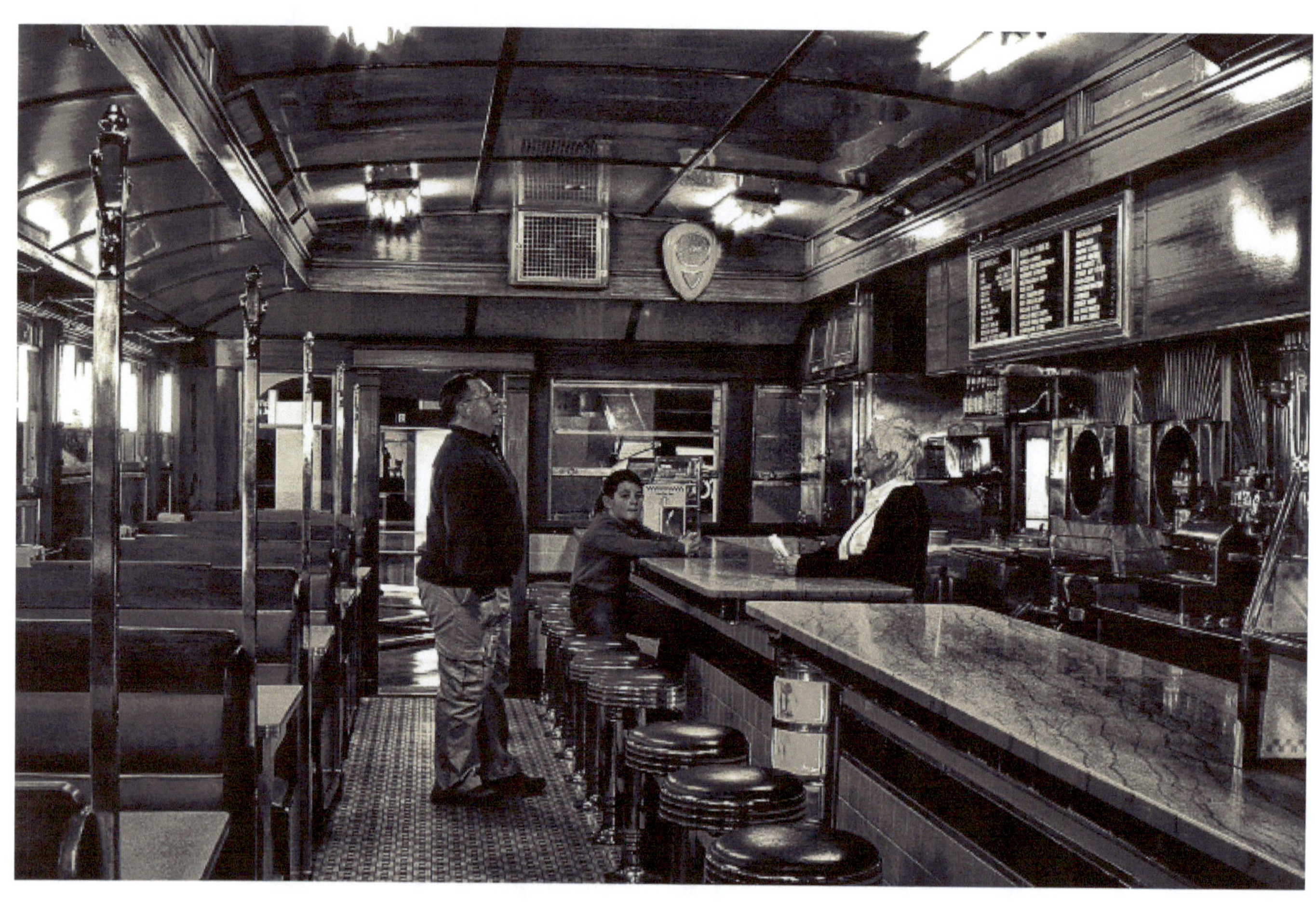

1940 Diner, Maurice W. Sanders

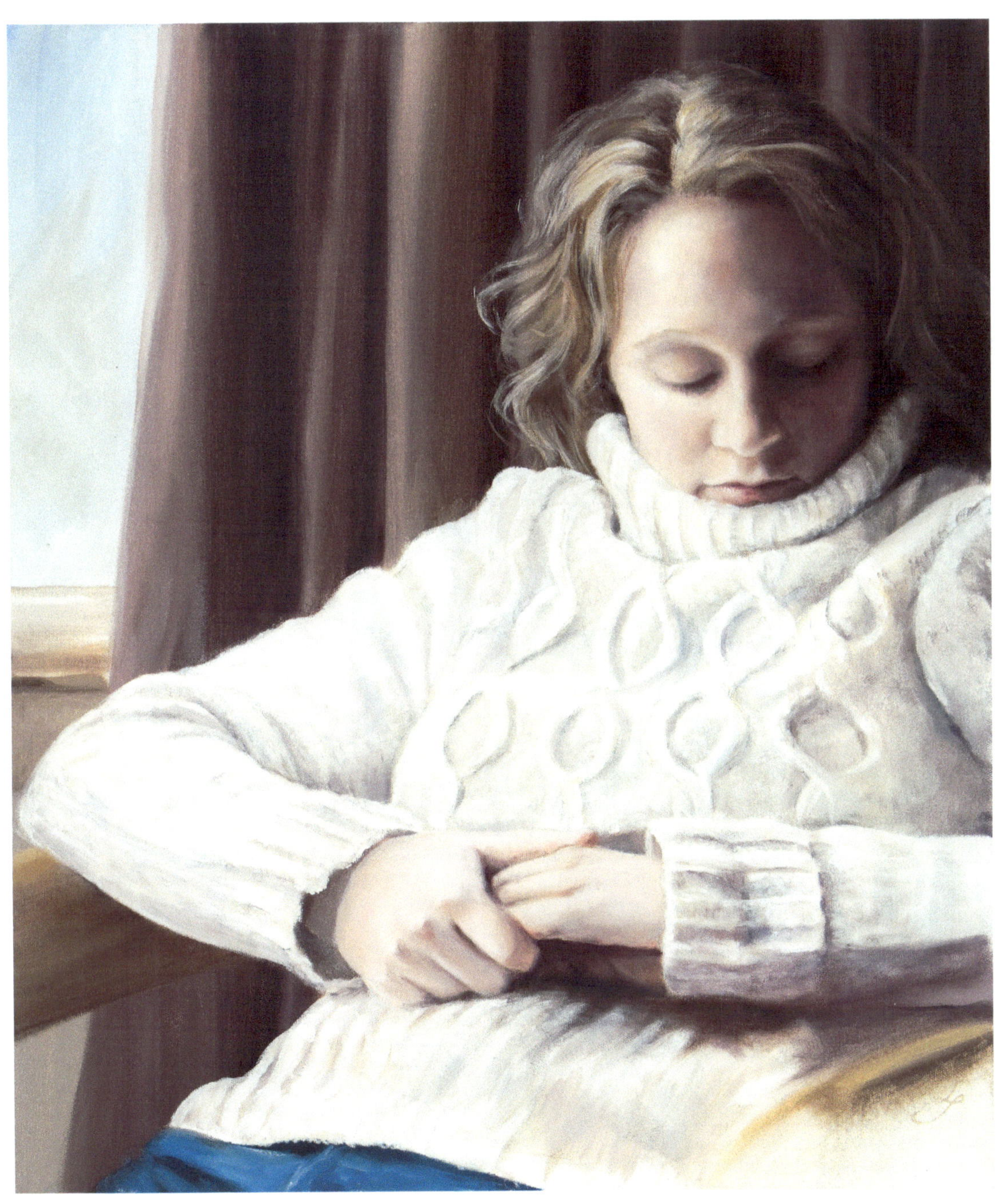

Aberdeen Dreams, Lois Primeau

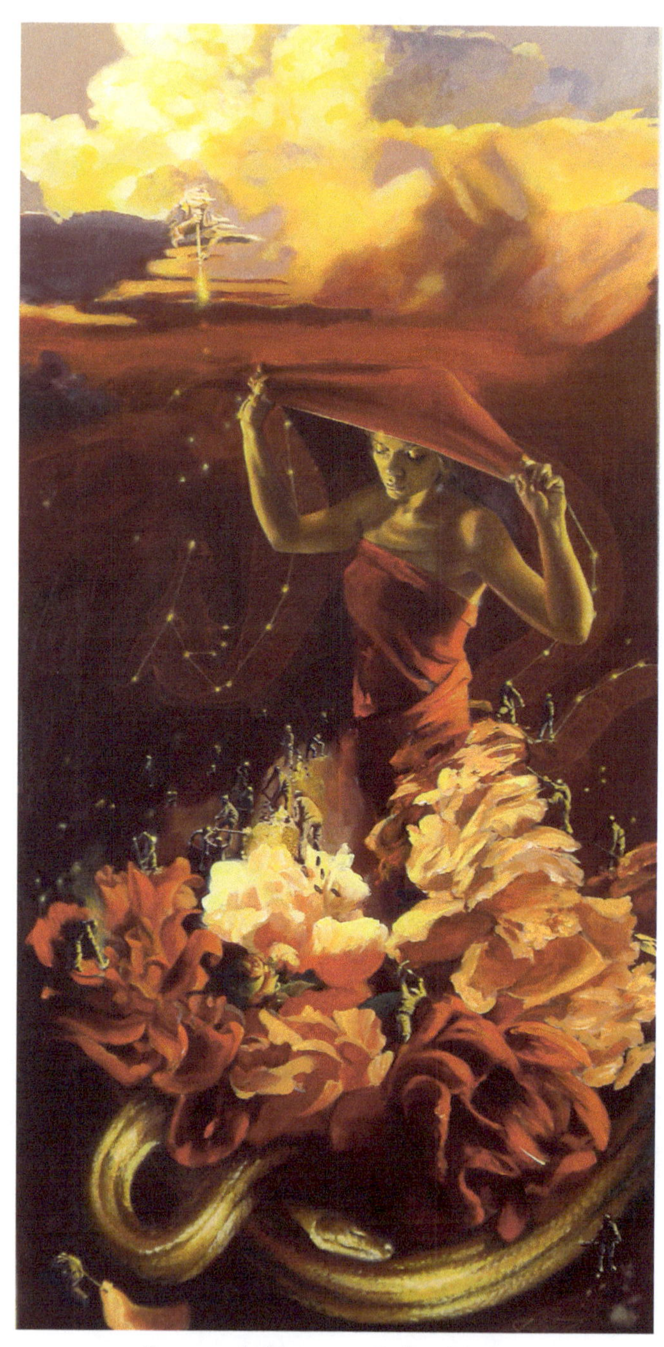

Serpent's Dream, Julie Zager

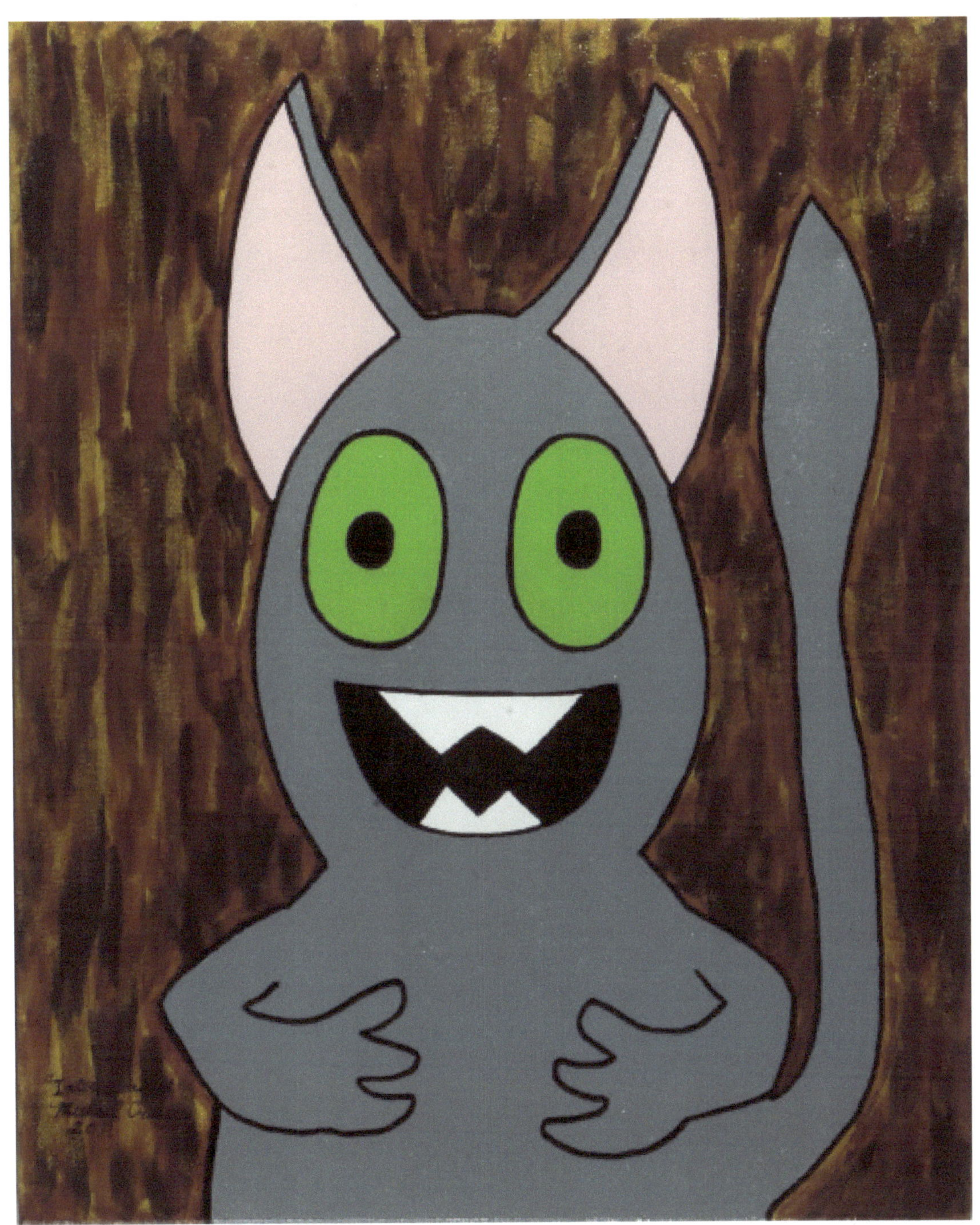

Frans Hals Cat, Michael Crane

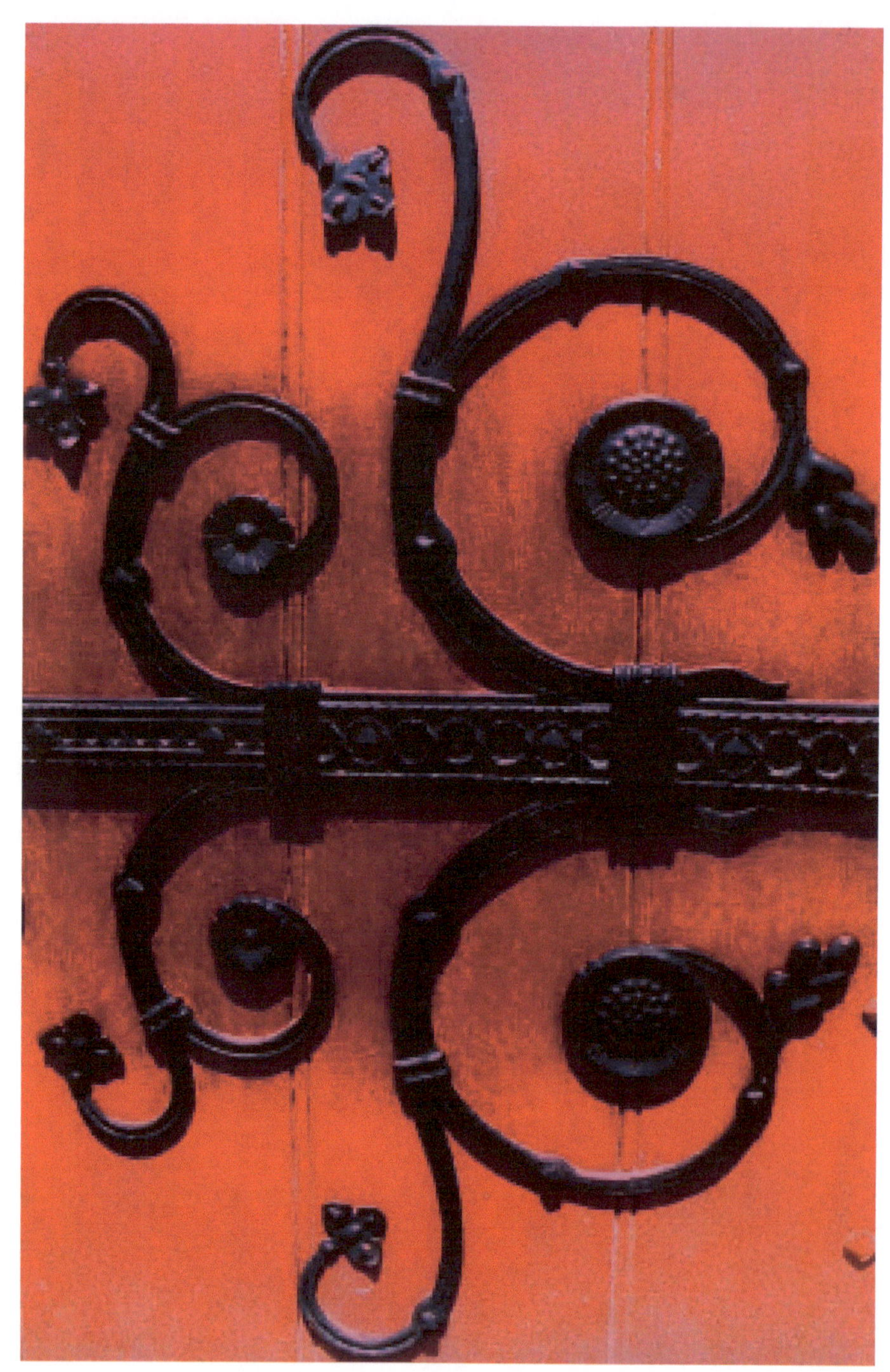

Iron Ivy, Lynn Jovick

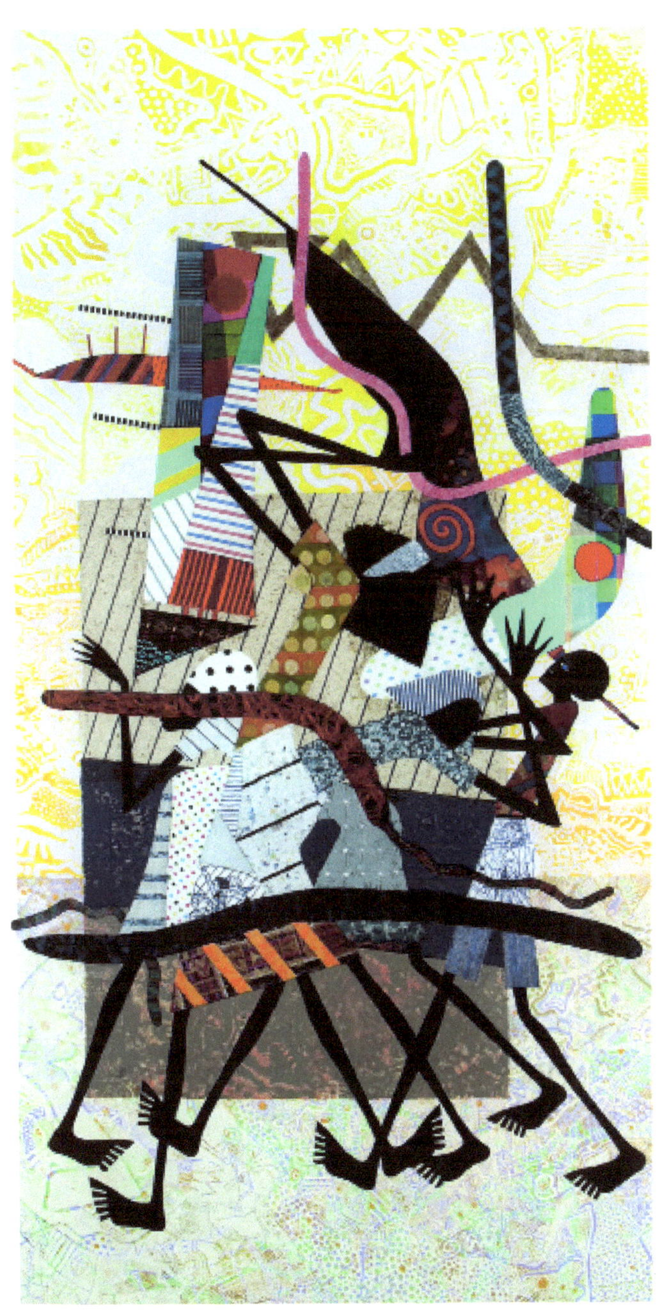

Play Patterns, Charles McGee

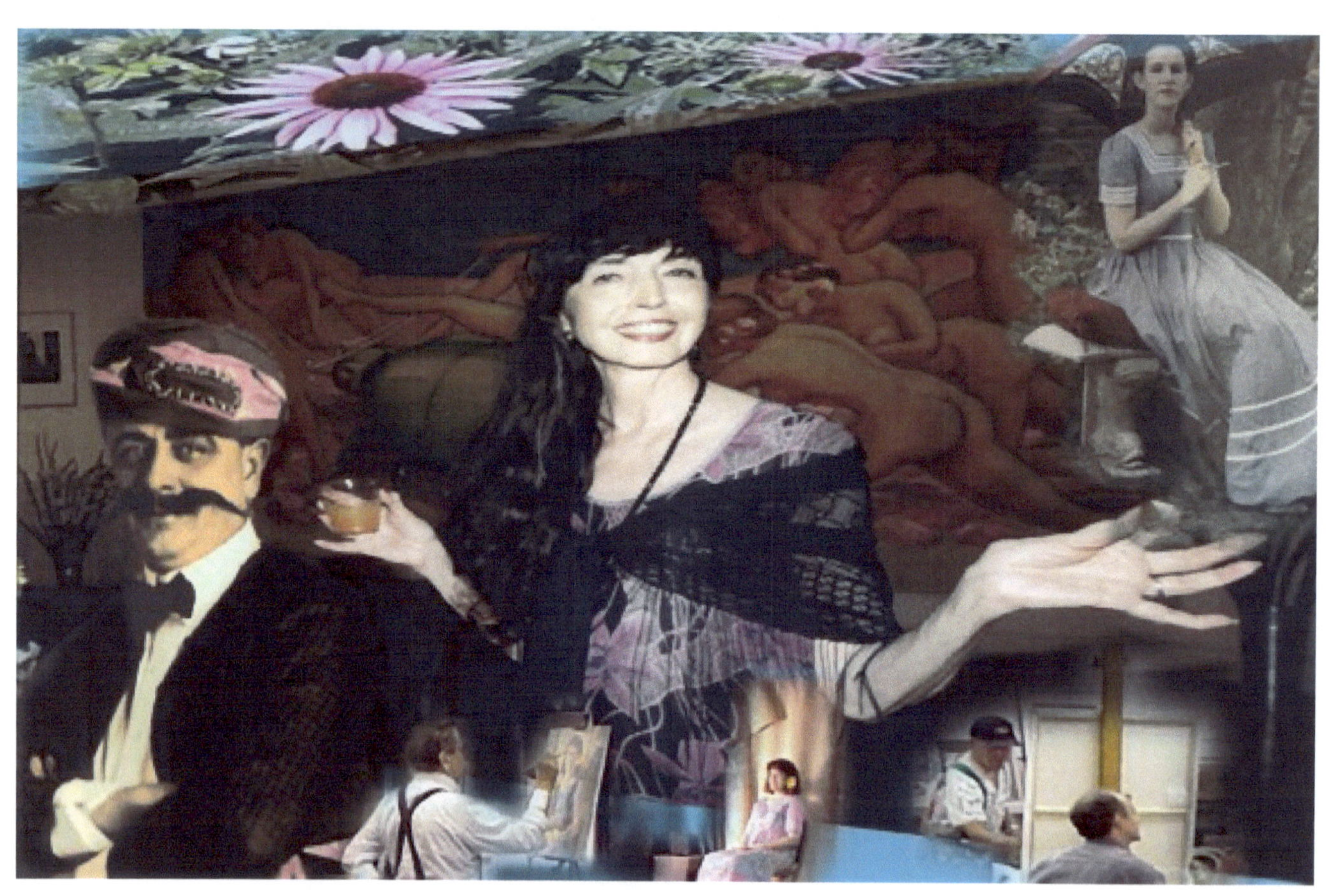

All This, George Booth

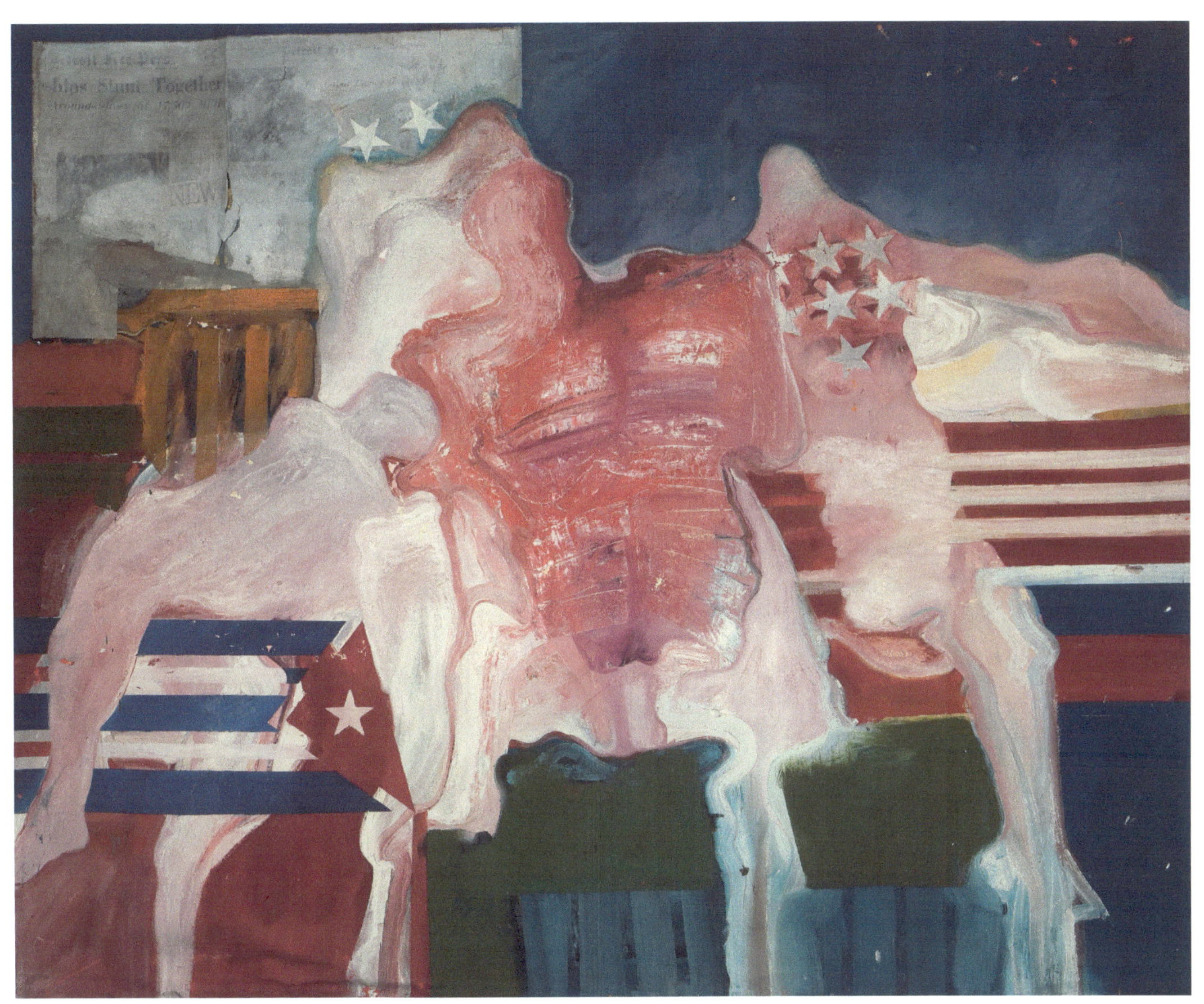

Prophecy of America, Pat Duff

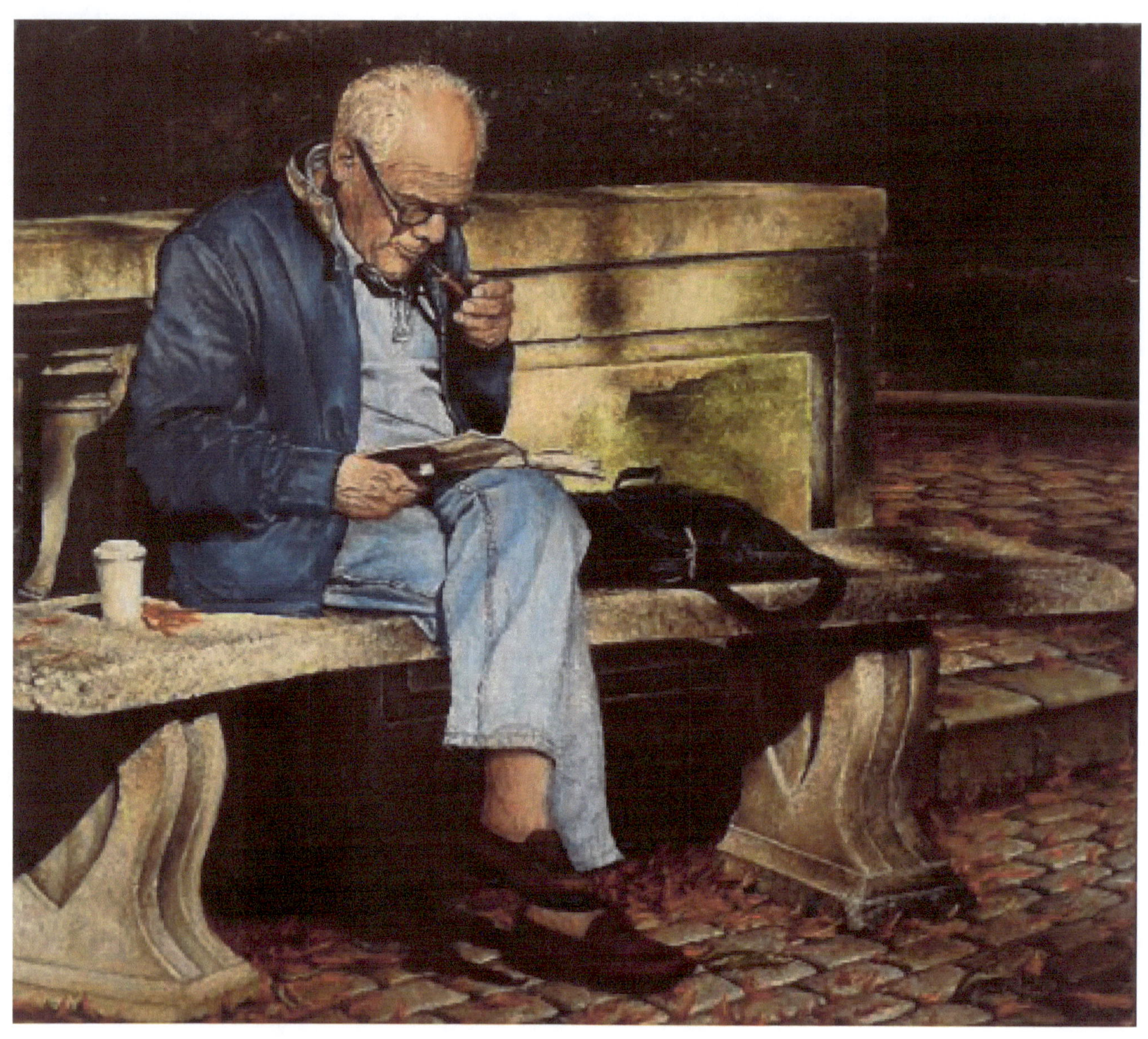

Autumn, Scott Maggart

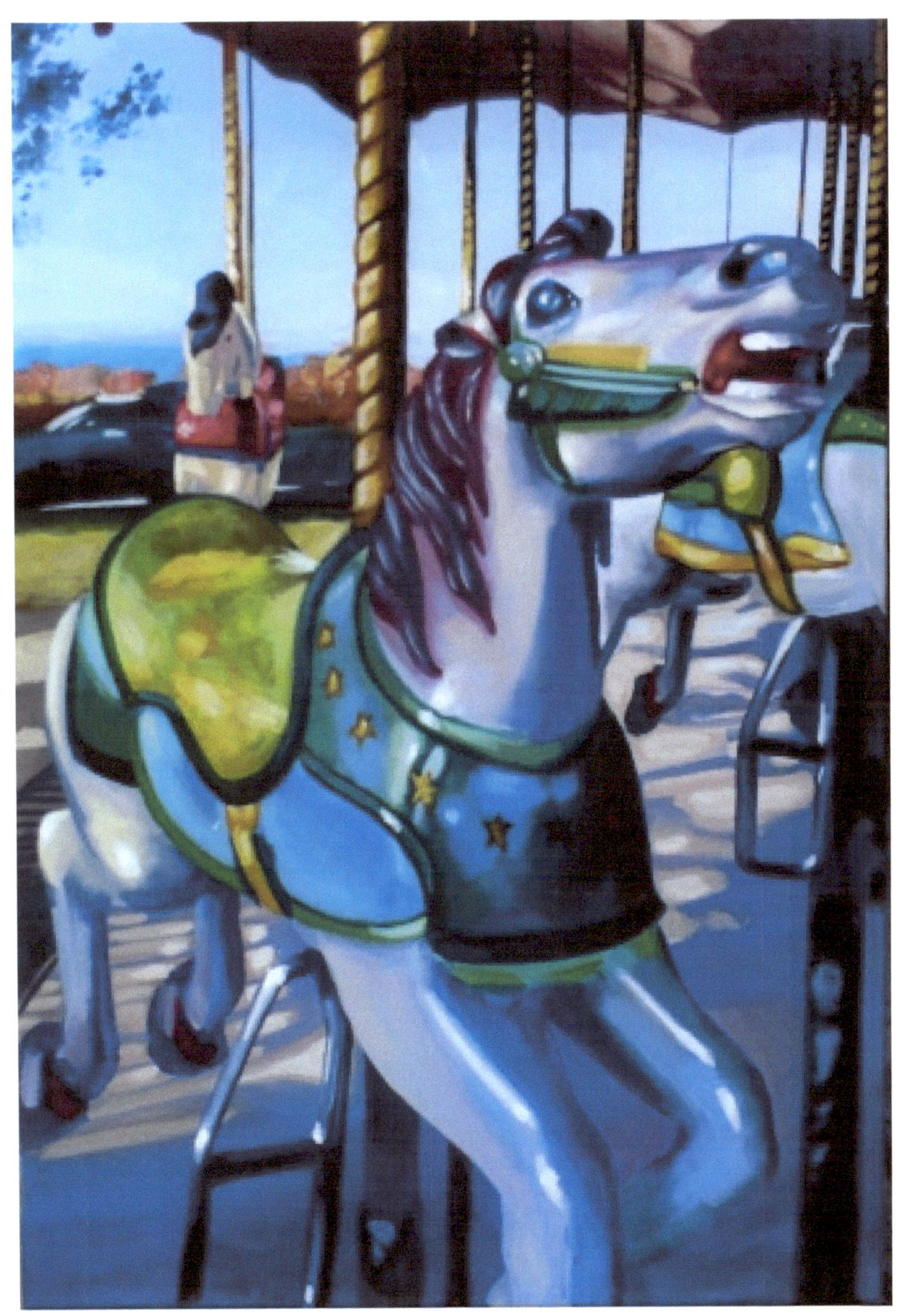

Crazy Horse, Mike McMath

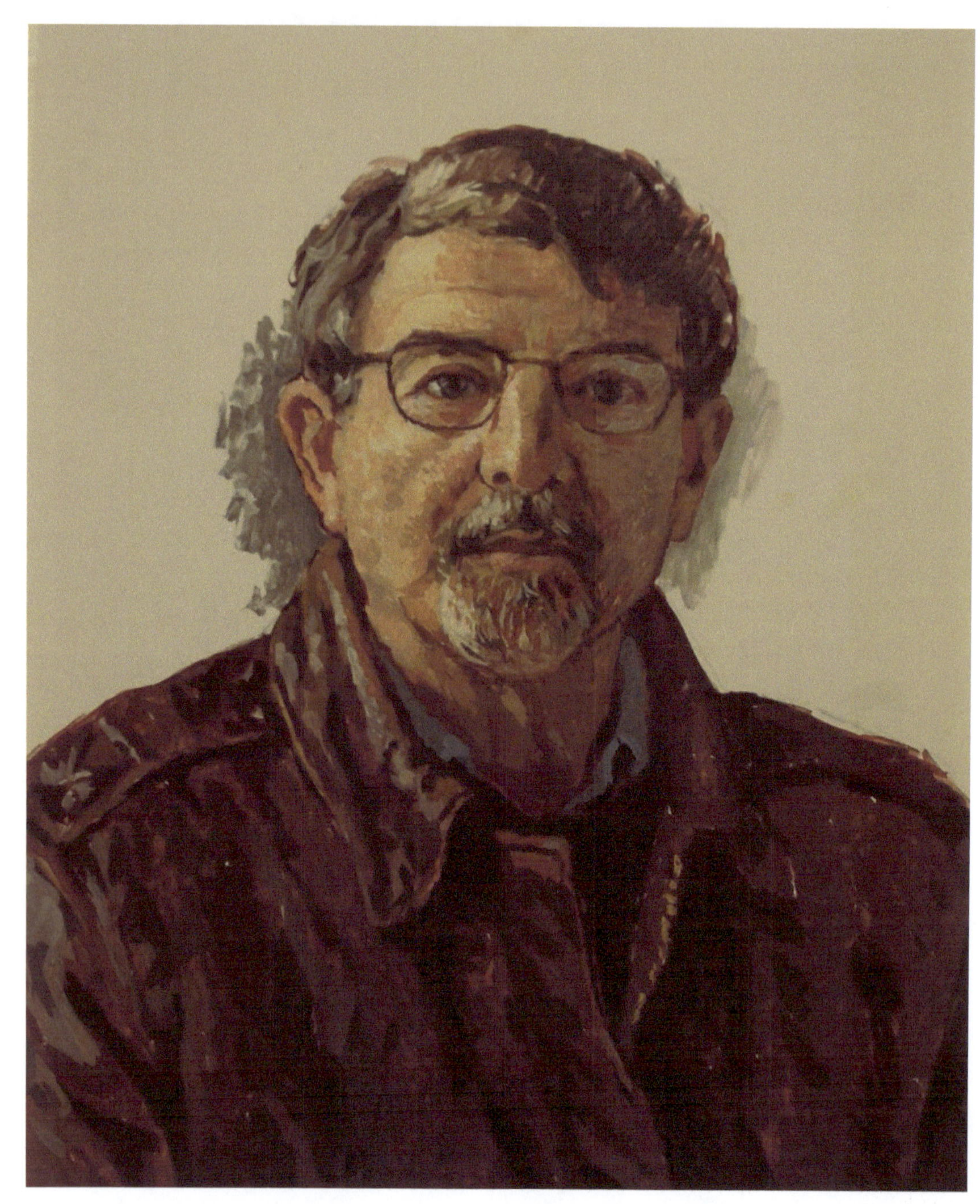

Self Portrait, Dennis Orlowski

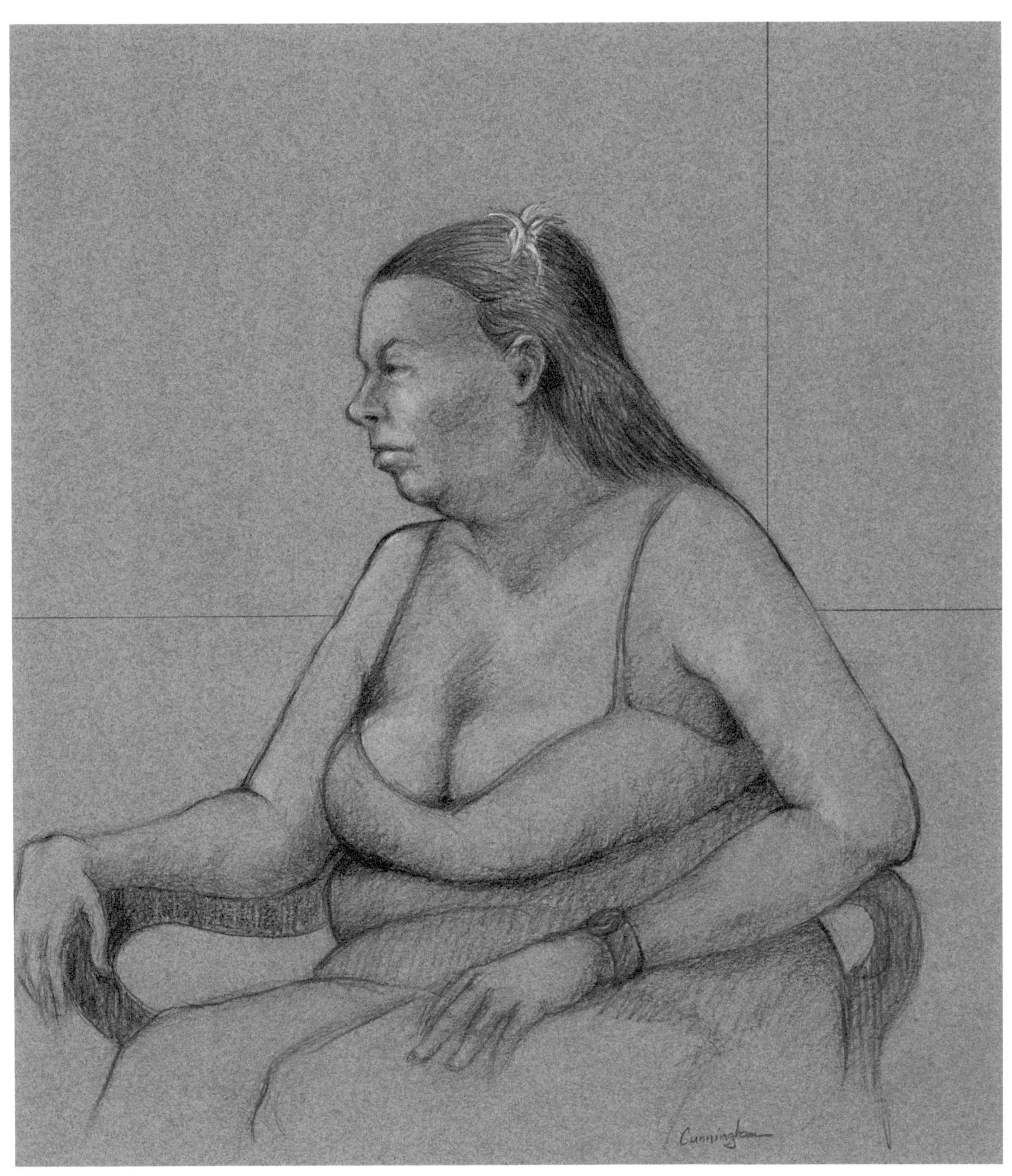

Florette, Tom Cunningham

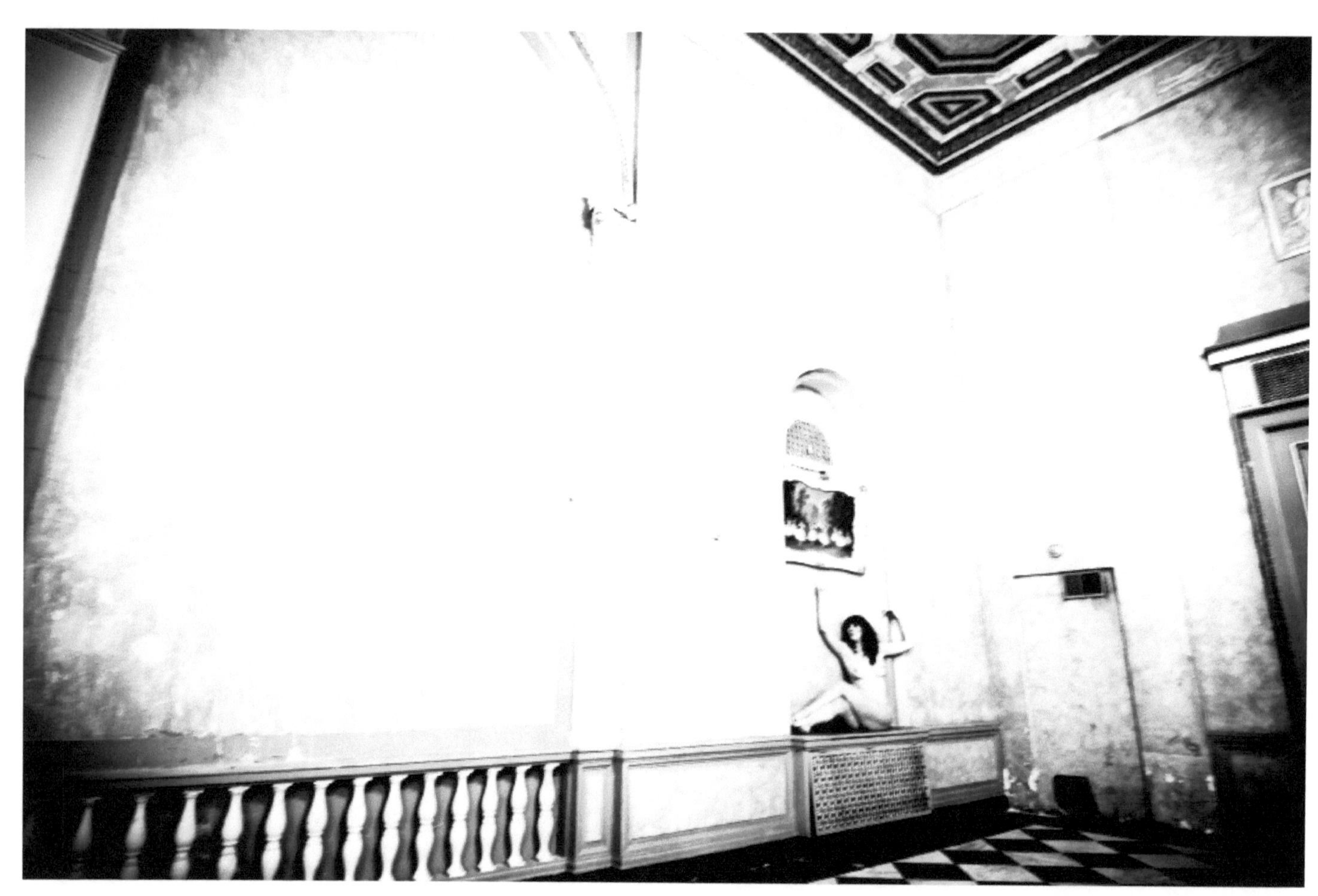

Adornment, bridgett ritz

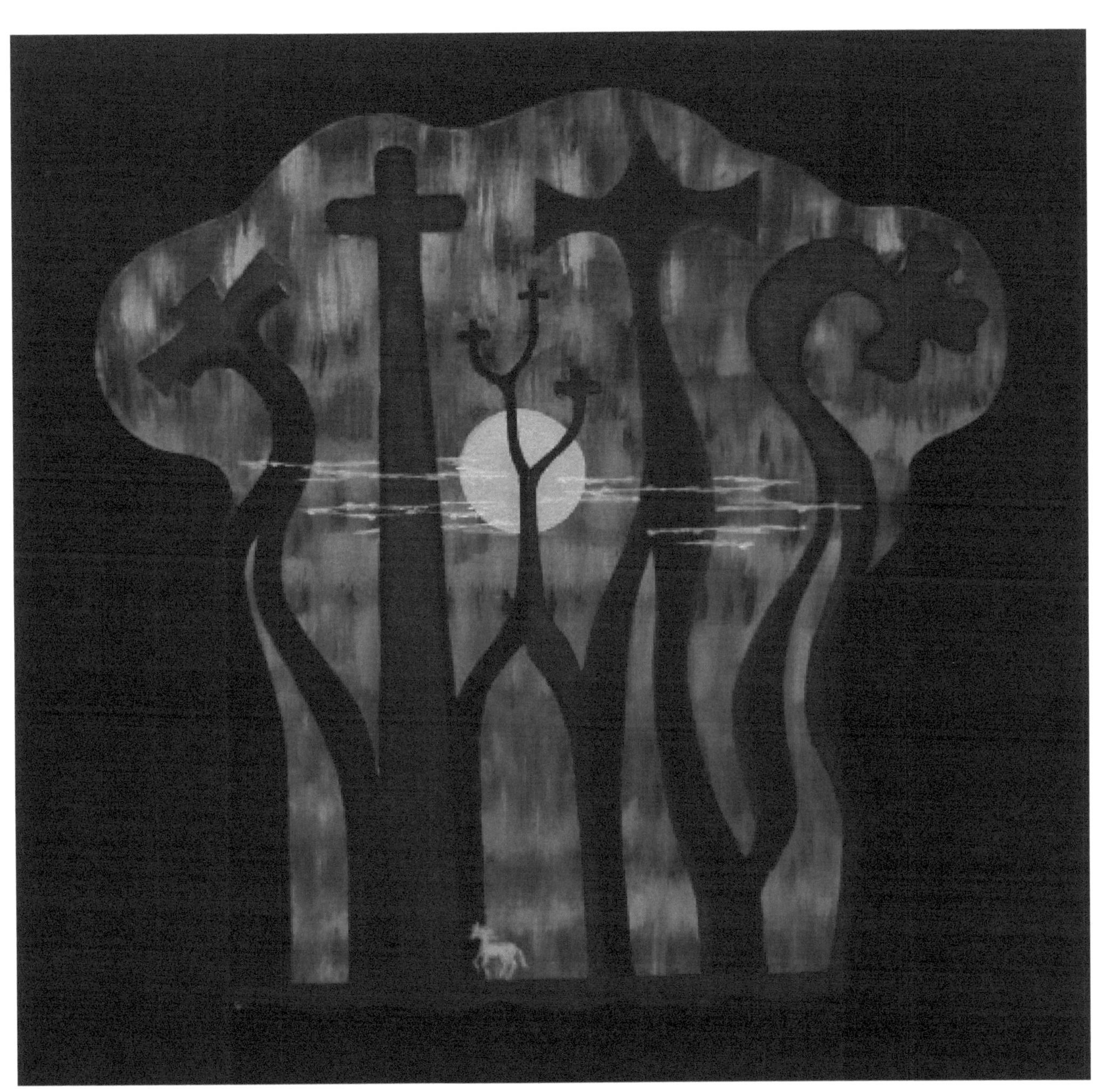

A Violet Nite in Cross Forest, Sherry Lynn Jolls

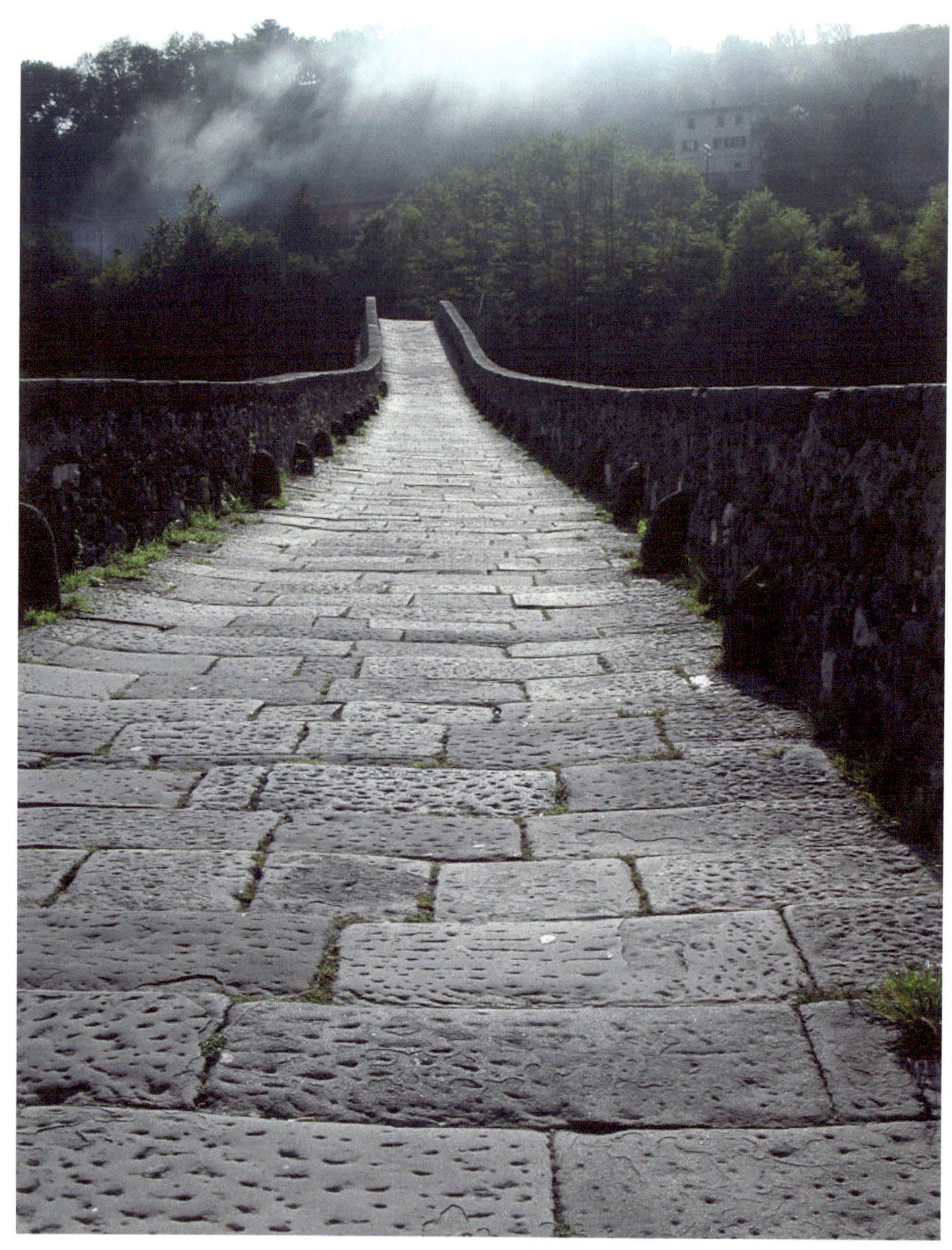

To......., Michael D. Goler

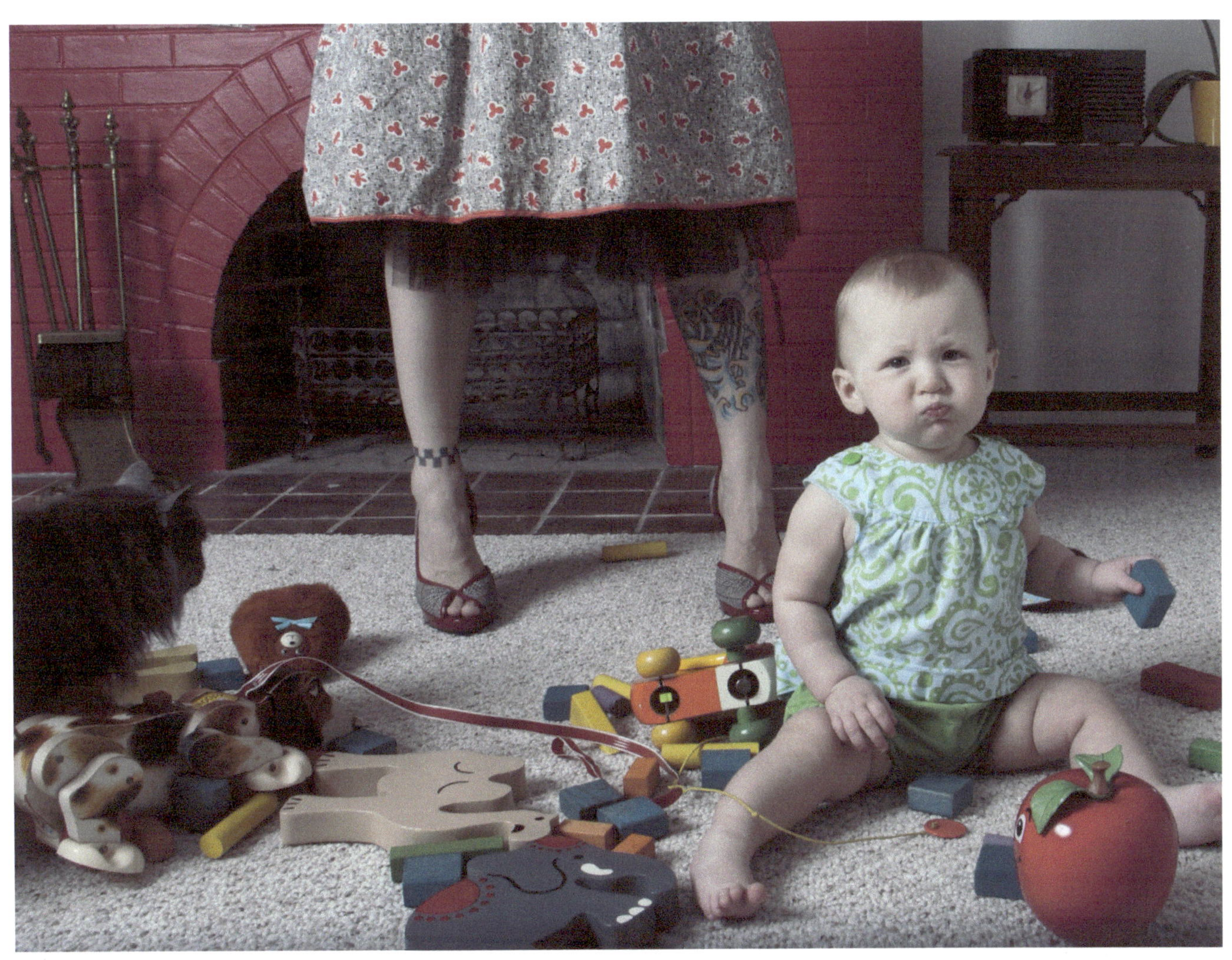

Untitled, Momcat Kelly

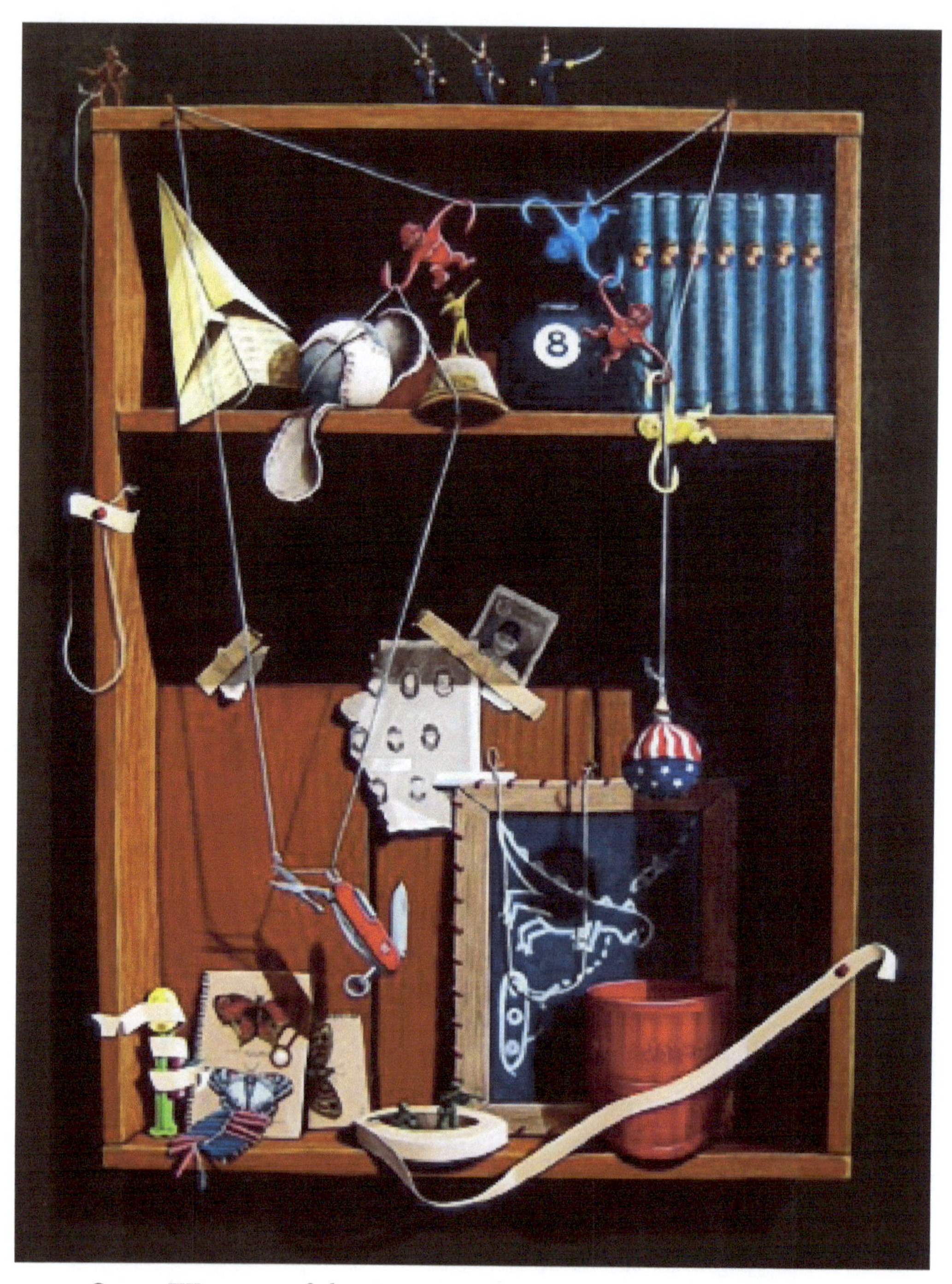

 Secret Weapons of the Attic Revolution, Joseph M. Neumann

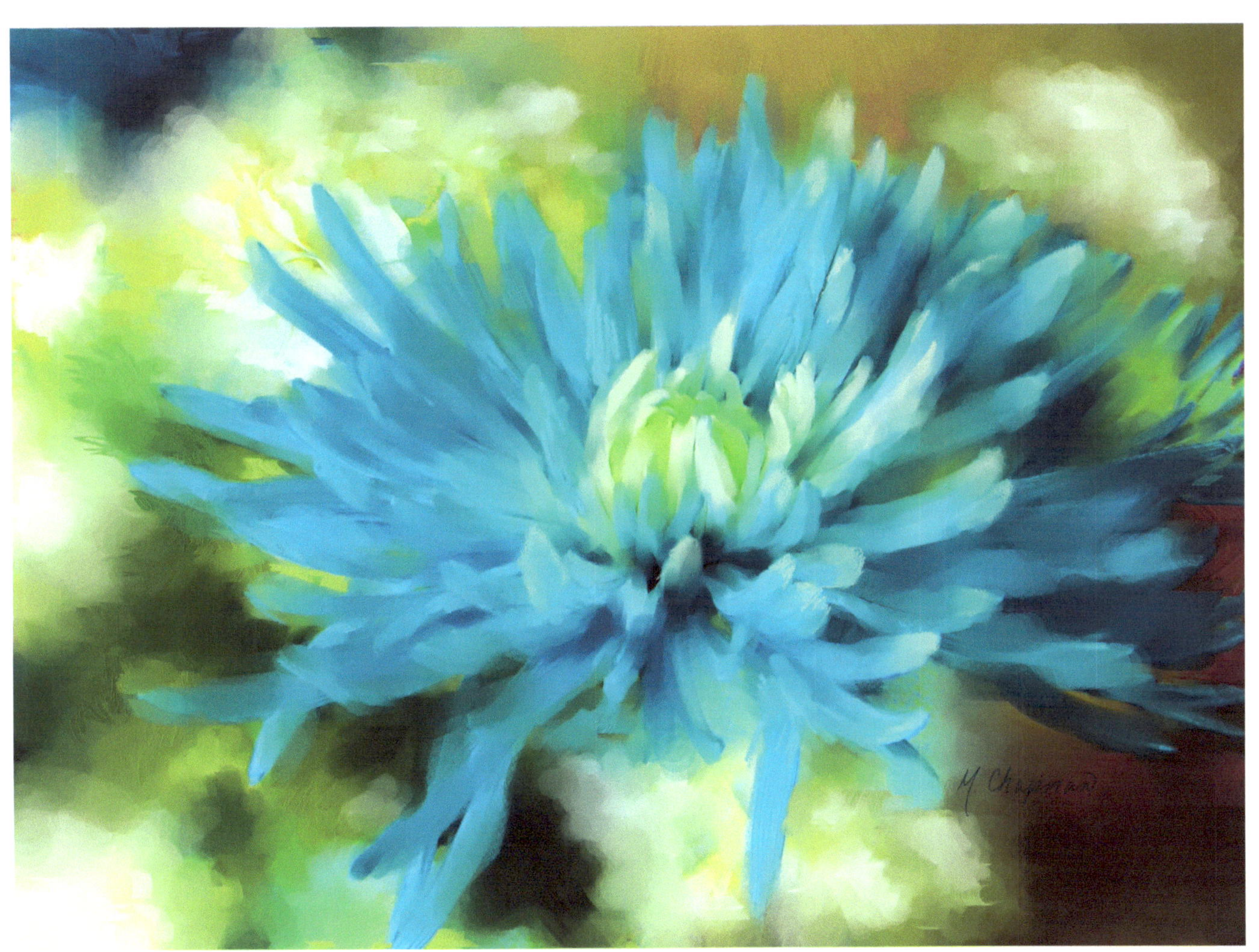

Blue Mum, Mardi Chapman

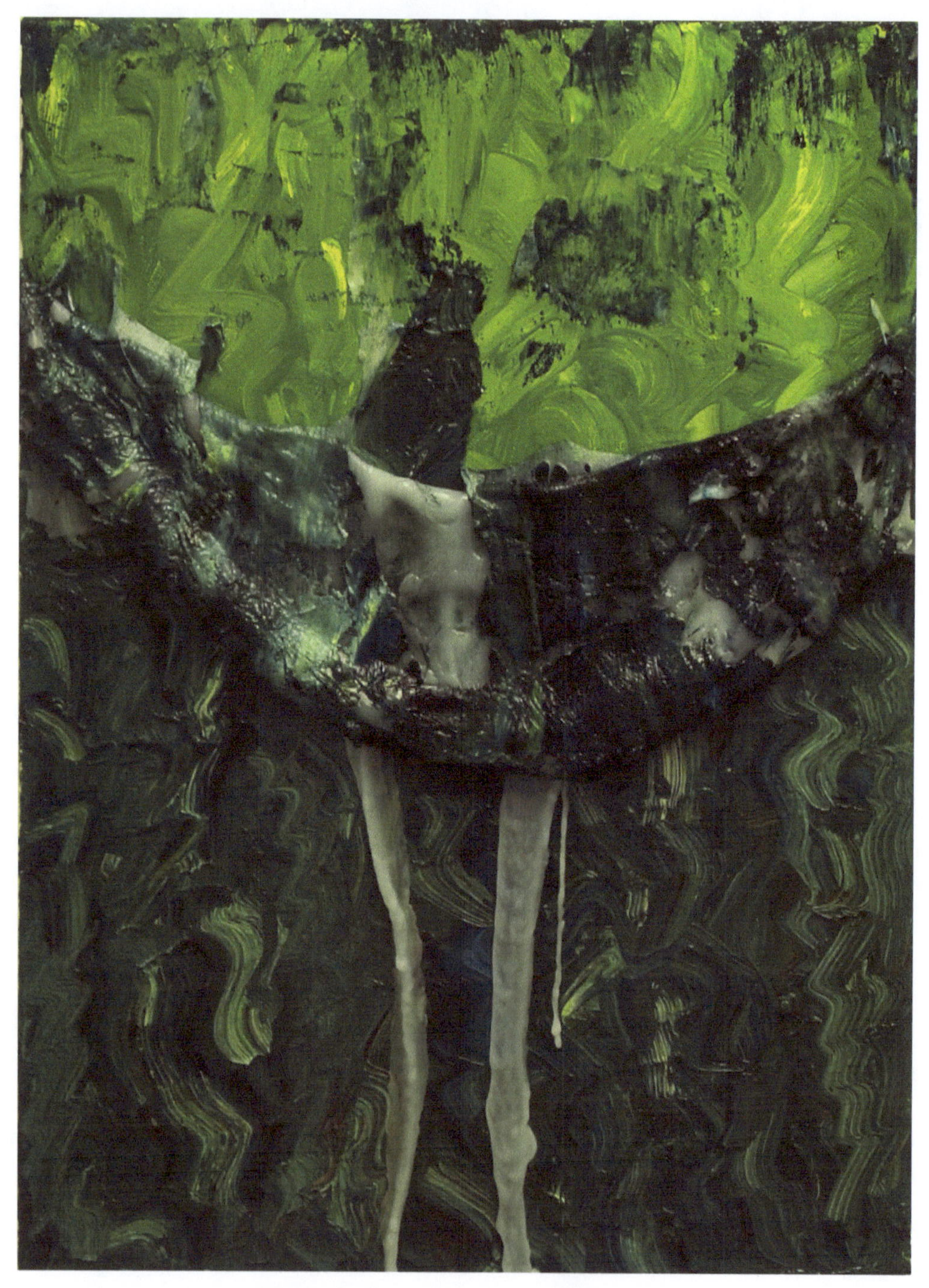

Path 10-1, Suzanne Sillery

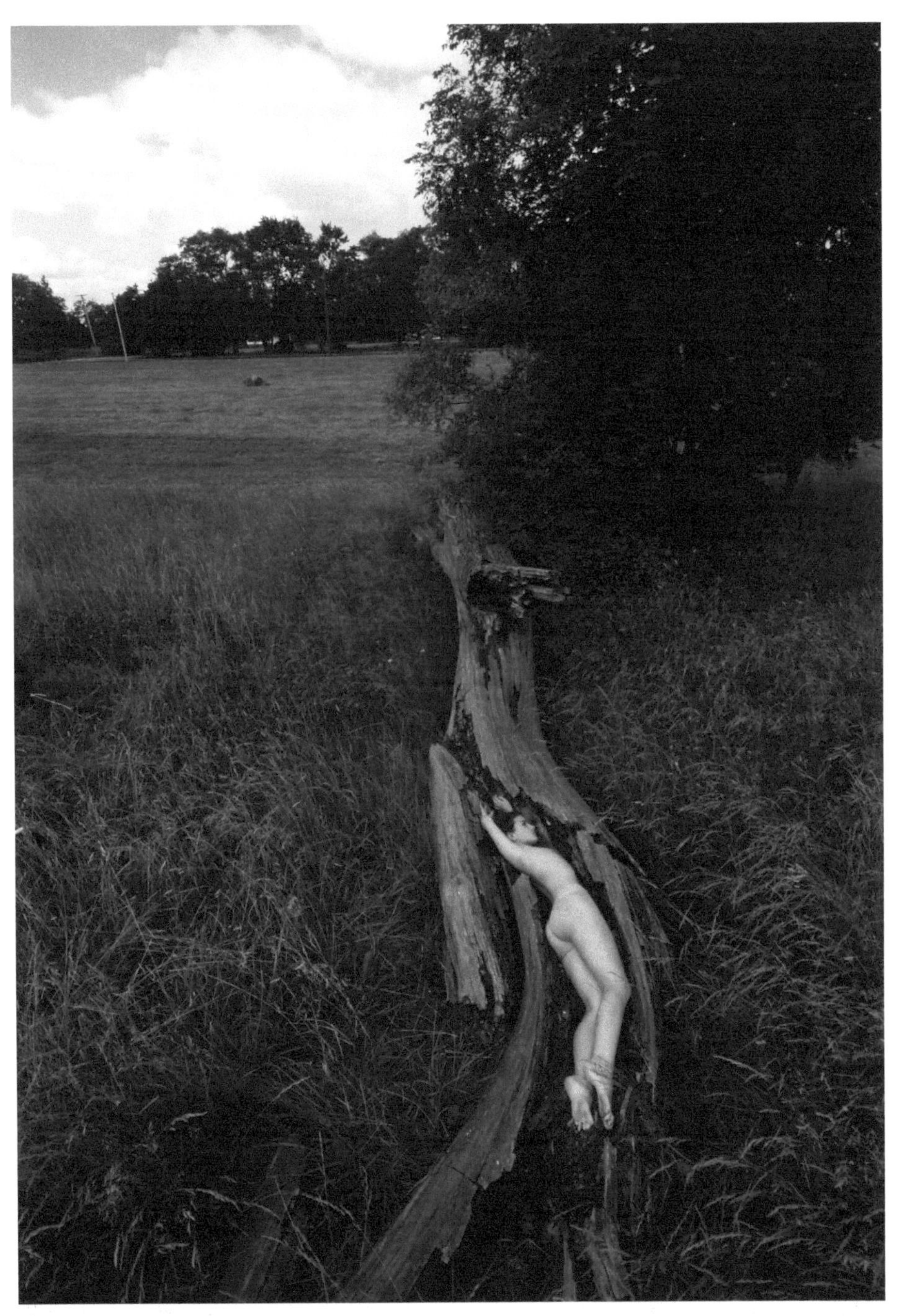

Fallen Tree Limb Nude, Paul Gomez

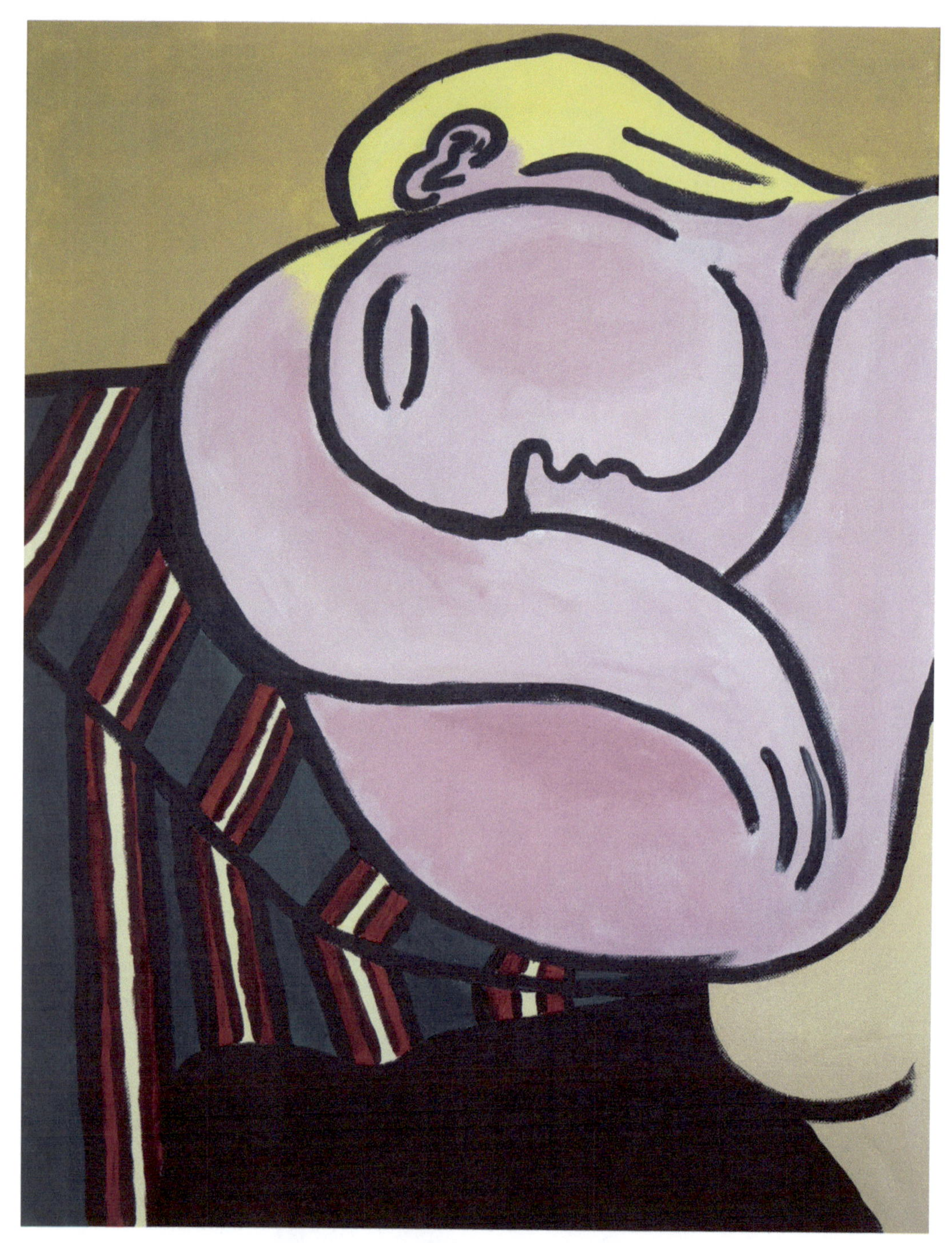

Woman Sleeping, Shelby Denton

Metier

Lou Cantoni

Working their favorite subjects,
some artists feature matt abstract,
others reach for a pale realism,
others do rheumy-eyed rhinoceroses,
and so it goes, an endless list.
With me, it's transcendent angels,
angels with wings, without wings,
especially my own omnipresent angel,
the one who speaks with me, whose name
is Light, who lights my path
even to eternity.

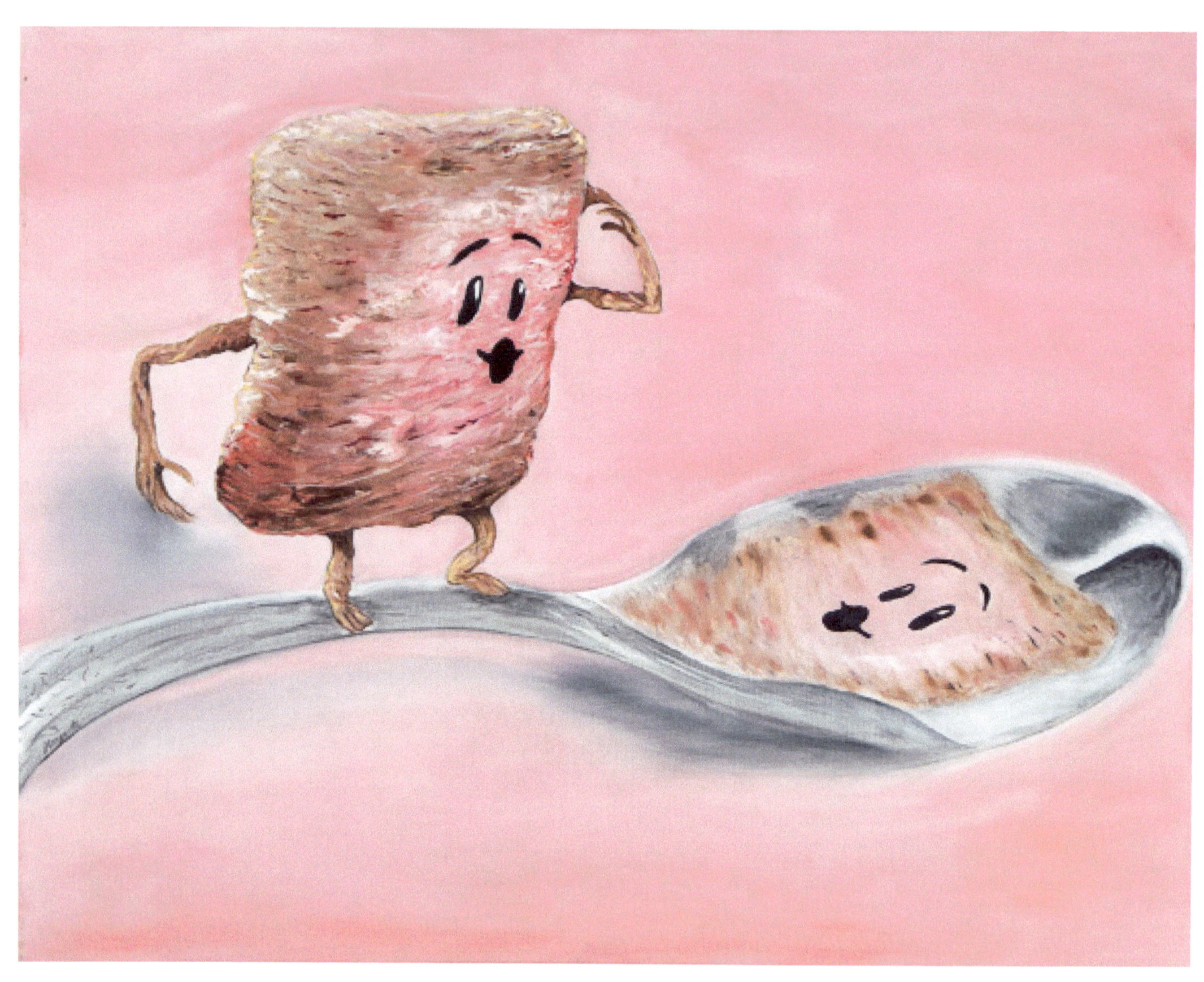

The Reflection, Margarita Beale

Belle Isle, Vincent Verna

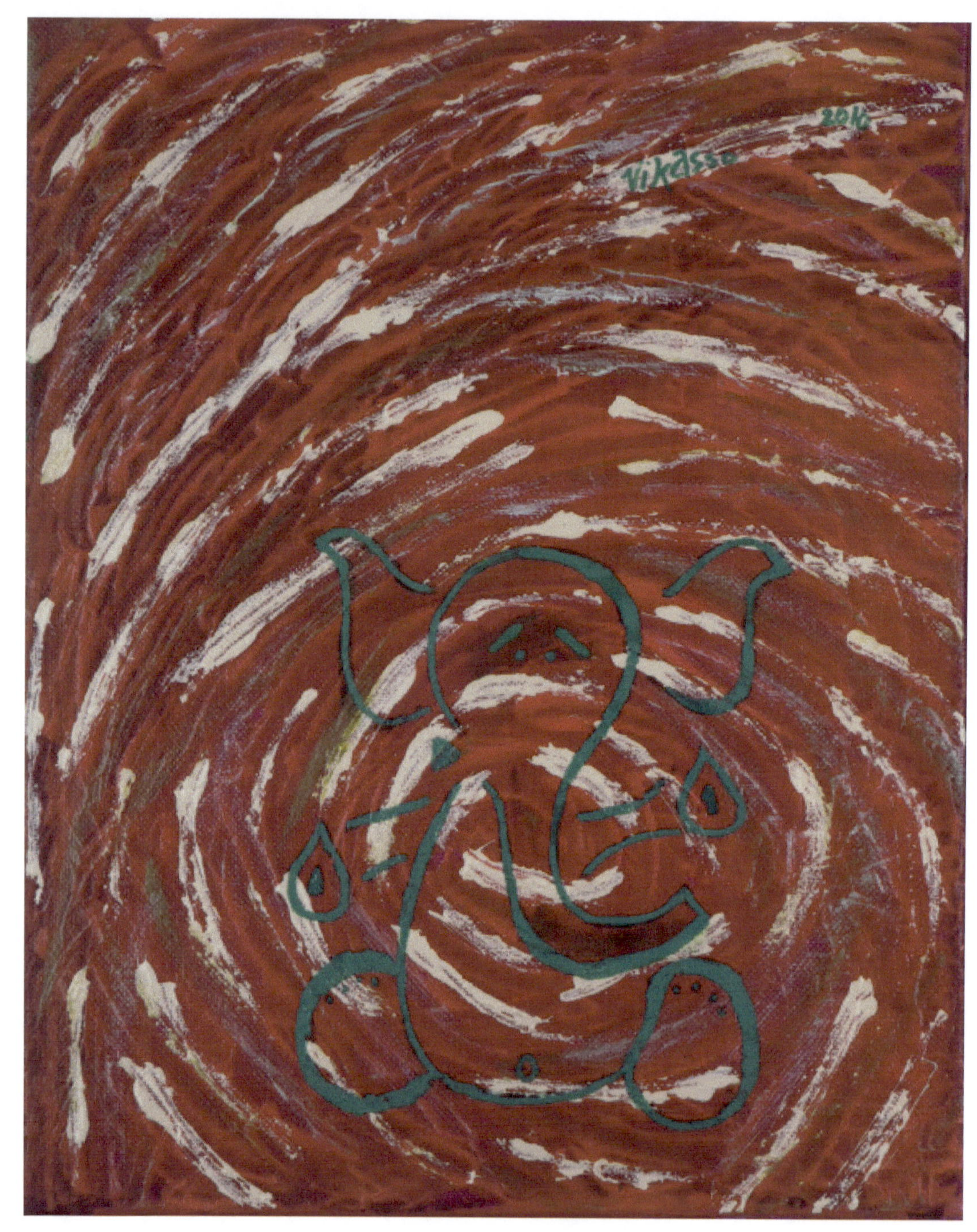

Untitled, Vikas Relan

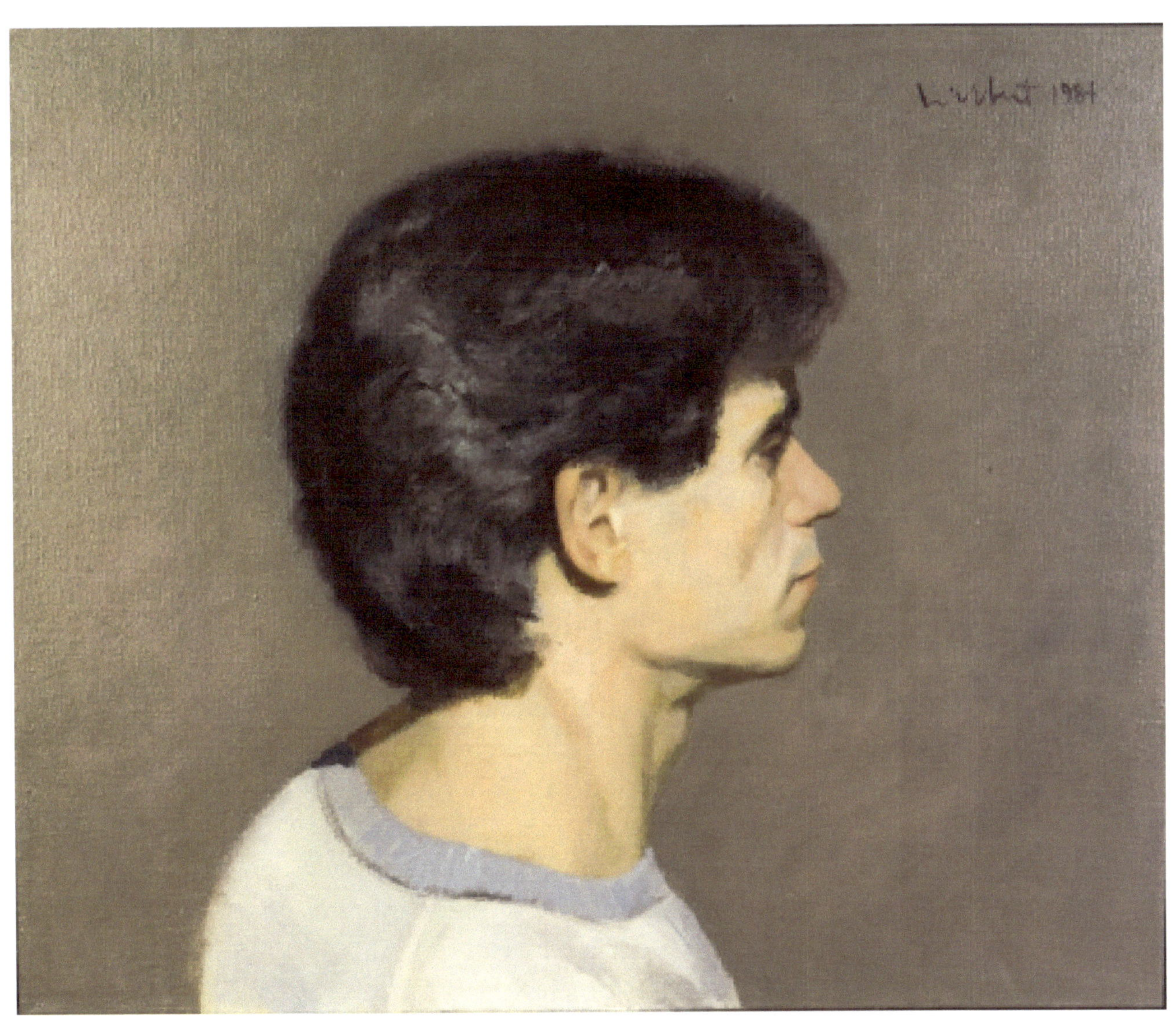

Mahoney 1, Robert Wilbert

To Ralph Waldo Emerson
(1803-1882)

Every generation has its heroes
Every literature has its giants
For American literature
You are one of its mighty mountains
Mighty like the sea, Powerful like the ocean
To you there was neither East nor West
Neither North nor South
I can almost hear the conversations
Between you and Thoreau
Between you and Whitman
You stood there tall as their Mentor
As an Oak Tree and a mighty Maple
As rock and the seas collide
What gave you such vision?
Being both seeker and the One sought after
One speech declared us all unique
Yet timeless
After you American Vision

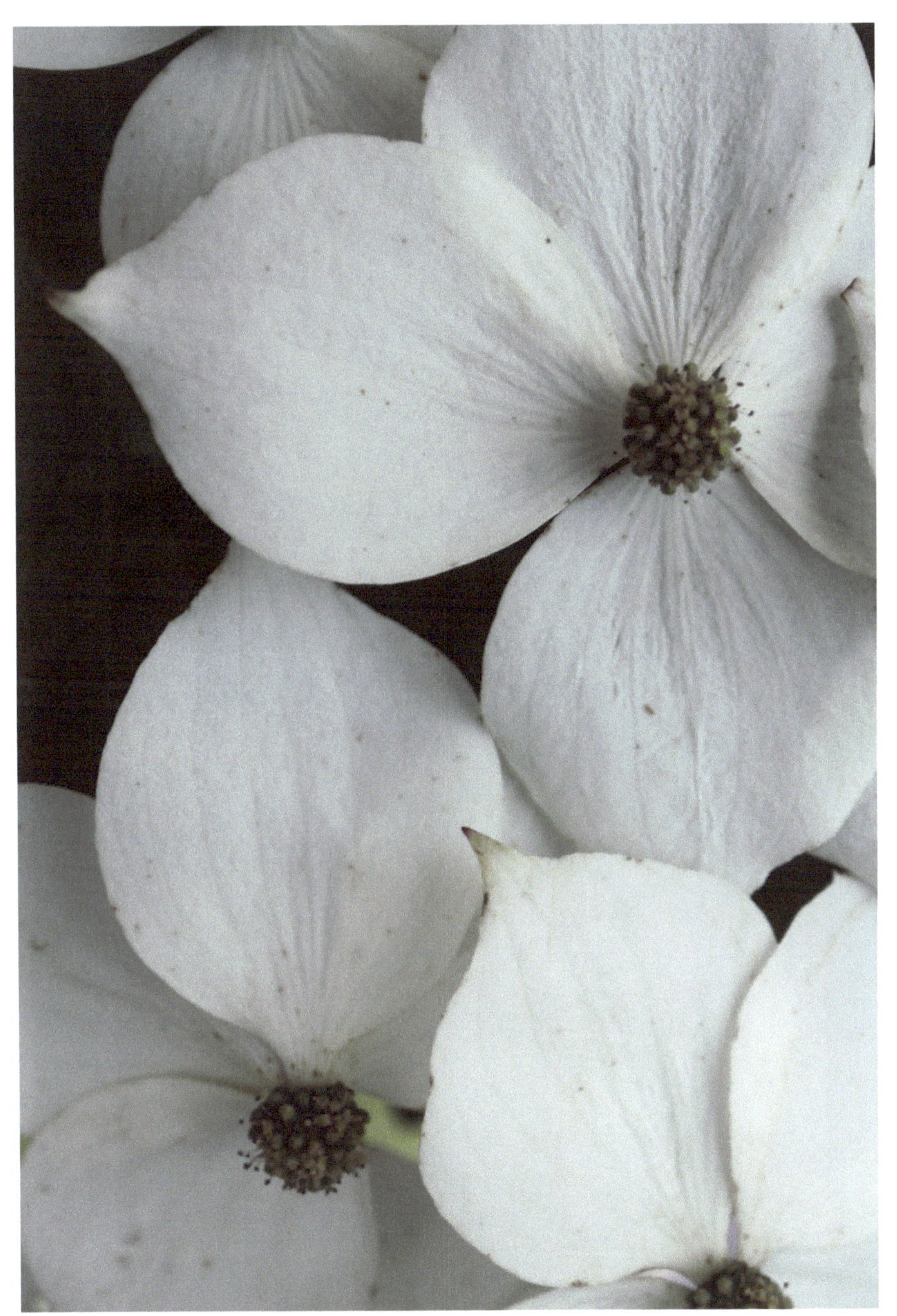

Dogwood Dream, Lynn Jovick

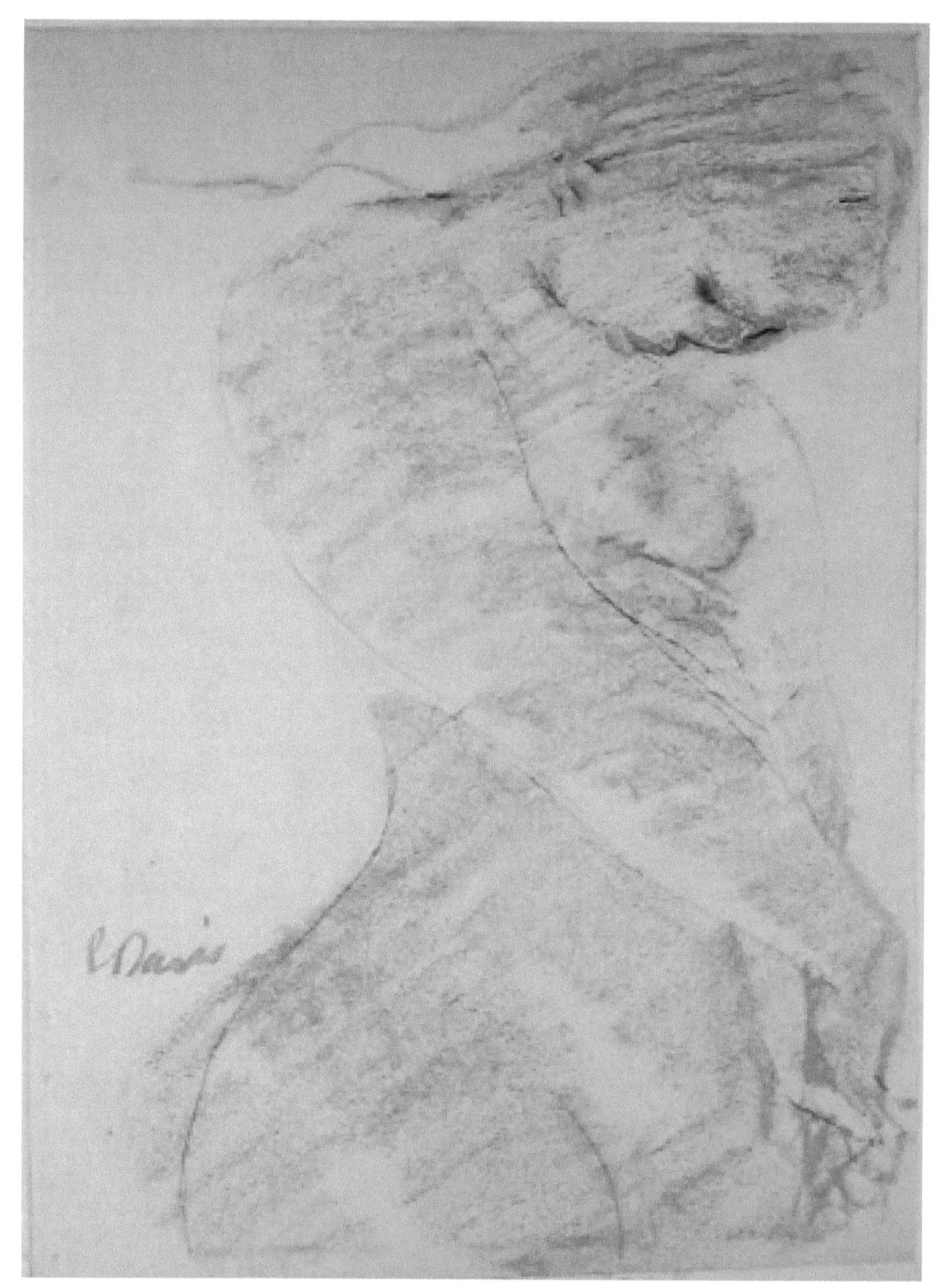

Eroica, Pablo Davis

INDEX OF ARTISTS

www.ingramcontent.com/pod-product-compliance
Lightning Source LLC
LaVergne TN
LVHW070128110826
845147LV00002B/208

* 9 7 8 1 1 0 5 2 0 1 7 4 5 *